Ground-breaking

HEALING RECIPES

for Modern Living

Anna Howard

Michael Terence Publishing

First published in paperback by
Michael Terence Publishing in 2019
http://mtp.agency

ISBN 9781912639793

This book would not have been possible without the support and encouragement of my wonderful family.

- Anna Howard

More at http://annahoward.co.uk

Contents

"A family is a place where minds come in contact with one another. If these minds love one another the home will be as beautiful as a flower garden."

- Buddha

About Anna

Anna Howard is an experienced, highly-qualified Reiki Master and natural health coach. In this book, she offers an alternative to over-fussy health foods, crowded, competitive fitness classes, complex meditation techniques and beauty and skincare products, laden with toxins and preservatives. Anna's ethos is all about living more naturally and she shows you how to use nutrition, exercise, natural healing and beauty to achieve balance in all aspects of your mind, body and soul. Through her natural beauty and mind, body and soul recipes, you'll find the help and resources to guide you on a journey towards feeling energized, balanced and healthy.

Background

Reiki Master, working with Reiki for 26 years

Stress Consultant MASC with 30 years experience

Qualified Yoga Teacher, 36 years of practicing Hatha Yoga

Qualified Beauty Specialist with over 10 years experience

Qualified Aromatherapist since 1987

Over 20 years researching food for healing

My Personal Story

This book has evolved from a lifetime of searching to feel healthy, vibrant and emotionally balanced. I was an unusually sensitive child and from an early age felt the impact of negative energies on both my mind and body. I could sense the presence of spirits and began to develop a high level of intuition. In my early twenties, due to this sensitivity, I started to suffer from anxiety and stress, which impacted negatively on my life. I lived in fear, lacking in confidence and balance, both physically and mentally. Instead of taking the medication quickly prescribed, I decided to search for a natural alternative approach, which was not widely accepted or available in the early '80s.

My journey to emotional and physical health began with the discovery of yoga at the Sivananda yoga centre in London. It is here that I learned the powerful message that our mind, body and spirit are all connected and balancing them leads to good health, mentally, physically and spiritually. Through working with the yoga poses and powerful breathing exercises, I found that I was able to bring my high levels of anxiety and stress back into balance and subsequently my health improved, along with my confidence and happiness. I began to feel great!

My health improved dramatically after a move to Portugal, where I was attuned to the universal healing energy of Usui Reiki 1 and a year later Reiki 2. I noticed the difference immediately and have never suffered an anxiety attack since the first attunement. I immediately started to use the gift of Reiki on myself, friends, family and even on animals with amazing results! Over many years of living in Europe and Asia, I have witnessed incredible healing with Reiki and Yoga.

I continued to investigate the importance of eating for a healthy body and mind and using foods as our medicine cabinet. This has evolved from a lifetime of food sensitivities, which caused so many physical symptoms. As a child, I suffered continuously with tonsillitis and colds, lacking in energy and stamina. After the birth of my son, I became intolerant to many foods and it was only when I began to remove the offending foods from my diet, that my health began to improve.

When I eventually returned to the UK, I decided to commit to Reiki and after a further two years of studying, I became a Reiki Master. I also trained in beauty, with a view to working with natural products for our skin.

I have been researching natural ways to balance our mind, body and soul for over 25 years and I have attended workshops, retreats, taken courses and run Reiki workshops. I have worked with so many people, all with differing challenges, from physical imbalances, to mental or spiritual challenges. On so many occasions, I have been amazed and incredibly grateful for the healing that has taken place and it's this healing that I want to share, through writing these recipes for the mind, body and soul.

"Change the way you look at things and the things you look at change."

- Dr Wayne Dyer

Balancing the Mind, Body and Soul

The Healthy Way Forward

This book is for anyone, who would like to wake up feeling healthy, energetic and balanced, with a deep sense of harmony within mind, body and soul.

There are so many natural health books, packed with instructions on exercises, healthiest food options, daily meditations and more. With such diverse information, it's understandable to become genuinely confused on how best to lead a healthy, balanced life. *"Do I need to eat chia seeds every day to be healthy?... I'm eating flax seeds every day, therefore, I am healthy...!"*

I feel that now is the time to take a different approach and adapt to a new spiritual way of living daily life. I have stripped it back and simplified the approach, offering a sensible, easy to follow foundation for a journey to sustaining a holistic lifestyle, that will improve physical and mental health, by balancing the mind, body and soul.

I believe that the way forward is to approach meals holistically, to consider the recipe, the qualities of the foods used in the recipe and how they support health. I invite you to consider how food is prepared, how it is eaten and even the ambience in which you eat.

I have then taken it further to embrace a spiritual practice and suggest powerful affirmations, yoga poses, meditations, visualisations and even skincare recipes all to support the healing properties of the recipe.

This is the next generation of recipe books, which has evolved from a frustration with the ways of preparing and eating life-giving food. In a world of quick fixes, fast food, fast eating, fast service, it seems you are supposed to be happy to eat prepared food on the run, food that has lived in a plastic container for days under the energy draining, bright lights of a supermarket, then heated up in an energy-zapping microwave. You are led to believe that this food will provide all the energy and the nutrients that you need to nurture and support your body. But of course, it doesn't and it can't.

It's vital for health that we approach meals and lead our lives, in a spiritual and holistic manner. The body, mind and soul all affect and influence each other and if one area is out of sync, then it is likely that everything else will be affected too. In this book, you'll find all the recipes you need to begin your journey to a balanced mind, body and soul, essential for good health and spiritual growth. You will also find recipes for beautiful natural oils and creams for the skin, plus recipes to calm and centre the mind and soul.

Food for Balancing the Mind, Body and Soul

How to Approach these Recipes

Prepare these recipes with respect, appreciation and gratitude

Food affects us emotionally and spiritually. Many lives have been healed and renewed through the power of wholesome, nutritious foods. It is because of its healing potential and spiritual energy that food should be sacred to us, prepared with respect and eaten with appreciation and gratitude.

Choose your foods intuitively

Approaching food intuitively is the key to eating spiritually. When you eat, try listening to your inner voice and ask: what does my body need today? Rather than: what do I want to eat today? In other words, how can I nourish and heal myself with the food I choose to eat? Listen to your soul and tune in to what your body needs at this moment and you will begin to make choices that will support your body and your health.

Choose locally produced food

Think about how far your food has traveled and

how many people have handled the food you are now eating. Food is energy and will be affected by others' energy too. Try to buy as much locally-produced food as possible, because this will limit the number of people or energies that have affected your food. If your avocado, for instance, has been handled by someone angry and unhappy, then this negative energy will affect the avocado.

Prepare calmly, with gratitude and positive intentions

Food is affected by all who touch it. Therefore, if you are well balanced and centred and prepare it with gratitude and love, this will send positive vibrations and energise that food. Food responds to emotions, so set your intention to prepare these recipes with positive thoughts, calmness, gratitude and appreciation for the benefits that healthy, nutritious food can bring.

Choose to eat less

Always be aware of how much you are eating and try to eat no more than two handfuls of food, so as not to overload the digestive system and thereby deplete energy. The aim is not to leave the table feeling heavy and sluggish.

Connecting spiritually

As you have prepared your food with love and thoughtfulness, it makes sense to make eating it a spiritual practice. I suggest playing some relaxing music, dimming the lighting, setting the table with love and care.

Try taking a few minutes to relax before eating. Close your eyes, take a few deep breaths and then focusing on the gentle flow of your breath, allow your body and mind to let go of all tension and relax.

Approach your meal with love, gratitude, appreciation of the ingredients and understanding of the healing energy of food. Treat it as a sacred rite, where food is transformed into strength, energy, love and light.

This connection to food is invaluable for strengthening mind, body and soul connection, thereby improving your chi or energy and health.

Mindful eating

Do you eat unconsciously, or quickly, instead of relaxing and enjoying the meal? The way you eat is as important as the food you eat. Mindful eating means slowing down and appreciating the flavours, textures and aromas of the food. Chewing slowly and well and enjoying it in a quiet setting, without feeling rushed or stressed.

Choose to eat nutritiously

There is little doubt that a poor diet, along with stress, toxic overload and not enough exercise, drains energy and creates an imbalance in the mind, body and soul. Energy, life force or Chi is the key to maintaining health and preventing disease. Eating nourishing foods, properly digested are two key ways to ignite energy.

Food is akin to daily medicine. Every fruit, vegetable, protein, carbohydrate or fat has a role to play in maintaining the body's health. It's vital therefore to aim to eat foods of higher nutrient density. Food can be extremely powerful. It heals and nourishes the body, tones the nervous system, calms the mind and strengthens the immunity system. It can even reduce wrinkles!

Fruits and vegetables are antioxidants and it is good to eat as many as possible. Try to include at least four varieties at every meal, focusing mainly on vegetables. Eating them raw is fine, except for broccoli or cauliflower. However, it's best to lightly steam all vegetables making them easier to digest. Plus, higher levels of nutrients are absorbed from some vegetables after they have been cooked.

Your Medicine Cabinet

Choose high energy foods to raise your vibration for a healthier, more balanced you

Apples the power of the apple! its anti-inflammatory properties make it invaluable to eat when you're faced with an illness.

Apricots amazing for rejuvenation, as they are loaded with minerals.

Asparagus packed with nutritional healing energy, their health benefits are vast and varied from supporting a pregnancy, treating tumors, boosting the health of the liver and balancing hormones.

Avocados easy to digest and excellent for soothing the gut and fighting inflammation.

Bananas a jealous fruit and best eaten alone! Powerful antiviral food and great for digestion.

Broccoli balances the hormones, boosts immunity and fights cancer.

Berries one of the healthiest fruits, loaded with anti-oxidants, vitamins and minerals, providing impressive health benefits, including being great for a healthy heart.

Cabbage great for healing and preventing headaches, constipation, stomach ulcers, arthritis, gout, Alzheimer's and heart disease.

Carrots impressive benefits include reducing cholesterol, lowering the risk of heart attacks, preventing certain cancers, improving vision and reducing the signs of premature ageing.

Cauliflower protecting and healing, said to the risk of cancer, heart and brain disorders.

Celery an invaluable source of antioxidants and beneficial enzymes along with vitamins and minerals, great in helping to lower cholesterol and reduce inflammation.

Cherries may protect against cancer, reduce inflammation and even slim your waist!

Cranberries low in calories and reduce the risk of urinary tract infections.

Dates have ancient healing powers from beautifying the skin to improving bone health.

Figs	the oldest fruits to be eaten by humans and a secret weapon for health issues, from preventing dementia to strengthening the digestive system.
Garlic	incredibly nutritious, low in calories, rich in vitamin C, vitamin B6 and manganese and contains trace amounts of various other nutrients.
Grapes	loaded with vitamins and minerals, so important for supporting a healthy balance body, mind and spirit.
Kale	has an abundance of health benefits, including detoxification, anti-inflammatory, cancer prevention and supporting the heart.
Kiwi	has over 20 vital nutrients and one of the most nutritious vitamin C foods around!
Leeks	an ancient superfood, packed with minerals and vitamins for a healthy body.
Limes	fantastic for weight loss, improving digestion and reducing respiratory and urinary disorders.
Mango	has amazing benefits from protecting against cancer to lowering cholesterol.

Melons strengthens the lungs and kidneys and a great energy booster.

Onions great for reducing inflammation and healing infections.

Papaya has powerful antioxidant effects, helping to fight cancer, improve heart health, reduce inflammation and even protect against skin damage.

Pears an ancient fruit with many healing benefits, from cancer prevention to improving digestion and healing the heart. Great for weight loss too!

Peppers rich in vitamins and antioxidants making them excellent for fighting disease.

Potatoes high in *fibre, potassium, vitamin C,* and *vitamin B6,* coupled with their lack of cholesterol, all support a healthy heart.

Squash fantastic for boosting the immune system, rich in vitamins and minerals.

Spinach fabulous for improving your skin and eyesight, regulates blood pressure and strengthens your heart.

Sweet Potatoes packed with nutrients and medicinal benefits such as managing diabetes, healing the heart and improving the skin and hair.

Watercress packed with nutrition, boosts immunity, prevents cancer and supports the thyroid.

Lentils and pulses help lower cholesterol and manage blood sugar levels.

Eggs power protein eggs have 8 major vitamins and a selection of minerals.

Brown Rice anti-inflammatory and fabulous for your heart, digestion, cholesterol and energy levels.

Quinoa an ancient grain, which has remarkable nutritional qualities as well as high in protein.

Oats a healthy grain, benefits include weight loss, lowering blood sugar levels and reducing the risk of heart disease.

Nuts studies have shown that people who eat nuts live longer than those who don't, which may be due to their ability to help prevent chronic diseases. (If possible soak in filtered water before eating).

Nut butters nutritious and loaded with health benefits; delicious on toasted rye bread.

Pumpkin seeds full of valuable nutrients and high in anti-oxidants, perfect for supporting a healthy heart and liver.

Sesame seeds an ancient food with wonderful health benefits.

Chia seeds packed with omega-3 and are a great addition to your smoothie or sprinkled on porridge.

Flax/hemp seeds a great source of protein, packed with health benefits especially for the heart and skin.

Cinnamon packed with antioxidants and may help lower blood sugar.

Ginger one of the healthiest spices on the planet, with powerful benefits for your body and brain.

Turmeric revered as a sacred root in India for its incredible health benefits; it is a powerful anti-inflammatory and a very strong antioxidant.

Olive oil amazing health benefits, a must for your food medicine cabinet.

Coconut oil a superfood and boosts immunity.

Coconut milk

Coconut cream

Raw honey anti-bacterial, anti-fungal and a great source of anti-oxidants. Soothes a throat, heals wounds and deals with digestive problems.

Apple cider great for promoting weight and body fat loss and lowering vinegar, blood sugar and insulin levels.

Spices your medicine cabinet, used in healing since ancient times.

Herbs wealth of medicinal qualities, fresh herbs make a lovely addition to every meal.

Organic dried fruit a power house of nutrients with amazing health benefits from protecting the heart to controlling thyroid. If possible, soak apricots, figs, dates, raisins in filtered water before eating.

Sustainable fish high in many important nutrients, protein, iodine and various vitamins and minerals. Fatty types of fish are also high in omega-3 fatty acids and vitamin D, to help protect against heart attacks and strokes.

Organic meat health benefits such as the elimination of skin diseases, strengthening the immune system, long-term energy, building and repairing of body tissues and protection of the body from infections.

Fermented foods essential for supporting your immune system. They help improve digestion by creating a healthy inner eco system, and they can be more potent and cheaper than probiotic supplements. They are ideal detoxifiers, so important now due to planet toxicity, they restore the acid/alkaline balance in the body. Include sauerkraut, kefir, yogurt, pickles regularly in your diet.

A Healing Approach

- Eat foods that have a high life force energy. Whenever possible, buy fresh, organic and locally sourced food. If you can't get hold of organic then soak your vegetables, salad or fruit in a homemade wash by adding 1tbsp of cider vinegar or lemon to a bowl of filtered water for a couple of minutes before using them.

- Avoid sugary foods, replacing them with dried, organic fruit. If you start to crave something sweet, then eat some organic sauerkraut as it should help alleviate these cravings.

- Avoid foods that have little or no life force energy, such as processed foods, frozen foods, takeaways and ready meals.

- Try not to re-heat food; eat food that is old or looks like it has lost its life force energy.

- Avoid using the microwave, as its high temperature destroys the life force energy of food.

- Avoid foods that you may be sensitive to.

The main culprits are usually wheat, dairy and sugar. Experiment with grains such as rye and spelt and perhaps replace cows' milk products with sheep's or goats' yogurt and cheese. Also try nut milk, such as almond, coconut and cashew nut. I recommend keeping a food journal to help you become aware of the foods that you may not be tolerating.

- Limit coffee to one or two cups a day.
- Introduce herb or fruit teas.
- Hydrate by sipping warm, filtered water with a slice of lemon, throughout the day.
- Avoid starving your body and aim to eat regularly, with lunch being your main meal and a lighter meal early evening. Aim to eat supper at around 6 pm and try not to eat later than 7.30 pm.
- If you suffer from weak digestion, try separating your carbohydrates and protein. Choosing a carbohydrate meal for lunch and eat your protein at night before 6 pm. Eat fruit separately from your starch or protein, preferably in the morning before breakfast.

- Invest in non-toxic cookware. Opt for glass, cast-iron or ceramic-lined saucepans and avoid Teflon and aluminium. If possible, also avoid using aluminium foil and cling film, but if you must use it then try to prevent it from touching the food.

- Store your food in glass storage containers, rather than plastic.

Toxic overload

There's real concern over the shockingly high levels of toxins and chemicals in the world. Pollution is now thought to be the silent killer. Not only is food sprayed with dangerous chemicals but there are thousands of chemicals in skincare products too. It's believed that as many as 515 potentially harmful chemicals are being absorbed each day, just from beauty products alone.

These dangerously high levels of toxicity place enormous stress on physical and mental health, creating an imbalance in the mind, body and soul, which then affects overall wellbeing and health.

I have been researching and using natural make

up and non-toxic beauty products for many years and have included some beautiful recipes for pure, preservative-free, gorgeous skincare, made from home-mixed aromatherapy oils and everyday ingredients.

Recipes

Try not to put too much stress on yourself, accept your journey without judgement. Be an onlooker to this journey and don't expect rapid results or to be perfect. Instead, always be gentle and kind to yourself.

How to use this book

Choose your recipe.

Mindfully repeat the affirmation throughout the day of cooking the recipe.

Appreciate the healing qualities of the recipe.

Before cooking, follow the preparation suggestions for each recipe.

After eating, follow the individual suggestions for the recipe to support its healing qualities.

Achieving good health is like a jigsaw puzzle, with many recipes for healing to bring about a balanced, healthy you.

Life force energy lifting aubergine and coconut curry

Affirmation

Life force energy runs through my whole body. I feel vibrant, enthusiastic and energised.

Effect on the mind, body and soul

This dish is not only full of nutrients, it is also so easy to digest with a cleansing, harmonising effect on the body.

Aubergines are abundant in prana, universal life force energy, they help nourish and balance the body both emotionally and physically. The aim is for a peaceful mind in control of a healthy body, with a balanced flow of energy between them.

The organic aubergine's high vibrational quality will support you on your spiritual path, increasing your own vibrational energy which is a positive step to balancing your mind, body and soul.

Preparation

Prepare with love. Hold the aubergine in your hand for a moment or two before cooking, to tune in to its life force energy.

To connect to the earth's grounding and

stabilizing energy, place a Preseli Bluestone crystal in the centre of your table, or on your worktop. This is the stone that the Stonehenge monuments are made from and it has a magnificent, ancient healing vibration. Stand outside, preferably with bare feet, holding the crystal in your open hand and allow yourself to connect to the vibration of the earth. Take a moment to visualise the earth's energy as a bright, white light, drawing up through the soles of your feet, through your entire body and into your crystal lying on the palm of your hand. Then return the crystal to your table, knowing that its healing energy will connect to you and your food.

Ingredients

Serves 2

3 tbsp organic desiccated coconut

1 tbsp sesame seeds

1 tsp cumin seeds

1tsp ground coriander

1 tbs coconut oil

I large onion sliced

4 cloves garlic chopped

1 green chilli thinly sliced

1 red pepper diced

½ tsp turmeric

1 medium organic aubergine cut into 2cm cubes

3 fresh tomatoes finely diced

1 tbsp tamarind paste

1 tbsp coconut honey, date sugar or agave syrup

200 ml organic vegetable stock

1 tbsp organic natural yogurt, sheep's yogurt works well

1 tbsp double cream

A handful of fresh coriander

Salt and black pepper

Method

In a frying pan, dry roast the coconut, sesame seeds, cumin seeds and ground coriander over medium heat for a minute or two, stirring continuously and taking care not to burn the spices. Then remove and set aside.

Heat the oil in shallow pan and gently fry the onion for 10 mins until soft and slightly caramelised. Add the garlic, chilli and red pepper, cover and cook for a further 5 mins. Then sprinkle in the turmeric and dry roast paste, cooking for a minute or two. Follow by stirring in the aubergine, tomatoes, tamarind paste, coconut sugar, vegetable stock and season with salt and black pepper.

Replace the lid and simmer gently for 15 mins or until the aubergines have softened. Remove from the heat and stir in the yogurt and cream, then check the seasoning.

Delicious served with apricot and pistachio brown rice and a handful of fresh coriander.

Apricot and pistachio brown rice

150 g brown rice cooked in filtered water with a tsp of ground turmeric and salt

I sliced onion

1 tbsp chopped organic apricots

1 tbsp finely chopped pistachios

A squeeze of unwaxed lemon juice

1 tbsp coconut oil

Heat a little coconut oil in a pan, then gently fry the onion for around 10 mins until slightly caramelised. Stir in the apricots and pistachio nuts, add a good squeeze of lemon juice before stirring in the rice. Season with salt.

Yoga pose to connect and increase life force energy

The tree pose Vrksasana, is perfect for grounding and steadying the mind, body and soul. With a focus on tapping into the earth's energy vibration, makes it one of the best energy boosters.

Stand in Tadasana, or mountain pose, focus your attention and weight onto your left foot, then bend your right knee, reaching down with your right hand and clasp your right ankle.

Bring your right foot up and place the sole against the inner left thigh, pressing the right heel into the inner left groin, toes pointing toward the floor. The centre of your pelvis should be directly over the left foot. (if you can't reach the inner left thigh then place your foot wherever is comfortable)

Bring your hands together in a prayer position in front of your heart chakra. Steady the pose and your mind, by staring at a fixed point around 4 – 5 feet in front of you.

Stay for around a minute and then step back to Tadasana with an exhalation and repeat for the same length of time on the other side.

Purifying and balancing beetroot and carrot salad

Affirmation

My body is cleansed, my mind is still, and my soul is pure. I am balanced in mind, body and soul.

Effect on the mind, body and soul

This is a quick and easy cleansing salad; perfect to eat anytime you've over indulged or are feeling sluggish and low in energy. Beetroot has valuable nutrients that support detoxification, lower your blood pressure, fight cancer and inflammation. Carrots have impressive health benefits from boosting immunity, protecting the heart and detoxifying the body. Eat this recipe to look and feel youthful and energetic.

Preparation

To prepare your body for the detoxifying energy of the ingredients, sit comfortably, preferably kneeling or crossed-legged, if possible. Take a moment to connect to your mind and body by inhaling through your nostrils to the count of 4 and exhaling for 4, repeat a couple of times. Then inhale for 4 counts, hold for 2, then lengthen your exhalation for 6 counts. Try a couple of rounds of this and if possible, try to lengthen your exhalation to 8 counts. A deep exhalation is a powerful tool in supporting the body's detoxification.

While preparing the salad, sip a glass of filtered water, which has been infused with a slice of ginger, lemon and cinnamon stick.

Ingredients

1 medium organic beetroot peeled and grated

1 large organic carrot peeled and grated

1 tbsp pumpkin seeds

1 tbsp walnuts roughly chopped

1 tbsp raisins

1 tbsp dried cranberries

Dressing

1 tbsp extra virgin olive oil

1 tbsp walnut oil

1 tbsp organic cider vinegar

1 tsp raw honey or agave syrup

A couple of handfuls fresh parsley finely chopped

Salt and black pepper

Method

Soak the raisins and cranberries in some filtered

boiling water for 3-5 mins, to lightly soften.

Meanwhile lightly toast the pumpkin seeds and walnuts in a dry hot frying pan for a minute or so. Drain the dried fruit, roughly chop then combine with the beetroot, carrot, pumpkin seeds and walnuts.

Whisk the dressing ingredients and pour over, giving a good stir to coat the vegetables in the dressing, then lightly stir in the fresh parsley.

Serve with a spoonful of tahini and date dressing for an energising light lunch, or as a delicious accompaniment to salmon.

Tahini and date dressing

1 heaped tbsp tahini paste

2 organic dates chopped

Juice from ½ lemon

1 tbsp filtered water

A good pinch of salt

2 tbsp Greek yogurt

Blend the tahini, dates, lemon juice, water and salt to make a paste. Place the paste in a dish, stir in the yogurt and drizzle with a little good extra virgin olive oil.

Also, makes a delicious accompaniment to garlicy lamb or chicken.

Meditative walk

After eating, enjoy a silent walk for 10 – 20 minutes, focus on the soles of your feet as you mindfully take each step, allowing you to tune in to the purifying energy of the earth. Should any thoughts enter your mind, gently accept them without judgement, allowing them to disappear by focusing again on each walking step. This is wonderfully calming and cleansing and will boost your energy and wellbeing.

Brightening and cleansing essence for the face and body

This healing essence brightens your aura and raises your vibration, to improve your mood, energise and invigorate the body, soul and mind. It will uplift the senses, promoting inner healing and a feeling of positivity, happiness and well-being.

1 small quartz crystal

50 ml of spring water

1 tsp aloe vera gel

2 drops of lemon oil

2 drops of orange oil

2 drops of geranium

5 drops of neroli

3 drops of lavender

3 drops of rose

Place all the ingredients in a sterilised spray bottle and give a good shake to thoroughly mix. Close your eyes, as you spritz over face and body and repeat the affirmation:

My body is cleansed, my mind is still, and my soul is pure. I am balanced in mind, body and soul.

Inhaling deeply three times, concentrating on each breath to feel supported throughout the day.

This will keep for a couple of days and is also lovely to use as a room spray.

Happy heart black bean and sweet potato chilli

Affirmation

My heart is filled with joy and gratitude; I am fulfilling my heart's desire.

Effect on the mind, body and soul

A nutritionally packed, tasty chilli, fantastic for boosting immunity. A dish to inspire feelings of gratitude and happiness, knowing that through eating it you are supporting your health and wellbeing. The ingredients in this recipe are believed to help balance blood pressure and blood sugars, strengthen the heart and even helping to prevent cancer. They also may have a positive effect on the nervous system, helping to prevent diseases such as Alzheimer's and Parkinson's.

This recipe brings peace and enhances the ability to see the way forward spiritually, enabling you to make important decisions for your journey to enlightenment.

Preparation

On the table, place a Green Aventurine, the perfect crystal for comforting and healing the heart. It clears, activates and protects the heart chakra to promote general well-being and emotional calm.

Place a few drops of Neroli oil in a small dish of water next to the crystal. This is wonderfully soothing and comforting to the heart and encourages the release of repressed emotions, allowing the healing energy of forgiveness to balance the heart chakra.

When it is open fully, the heart chakra becomes what the Buddhists call Mahakaruna, a channel for universal compassion—your true self. It is here where you invite this infinite love to flow through you, allowing it to heal yourself and others.

Ingredients

Serves 4

400 ml organic black beans, drained and washed with filtered water

2 tbsp extra virgin olive oil

1 large red onion peeled and sliced

1 organic sweet potato peeled and cut into 1-inch dice

1 red pepper diced

3 – 4 garlic cloves finely chopped

1 fresh red chilli finely chopped

2 tsp smoked paprika

2 tsp cumin powder

¼ tsp red chilli powder

2 large fresh tomatoes finely chopped

400g organic tin of tomatoes chopped

1 tbsp sundried tomato paste

3 tsp agave syrup

1 tbsp chopped green pitted olives

Juice ½ lime

Salt

200 ml of organic vegetable stock

Method

Heat the olive oil in a non-stick saucepan. Add the sliced onions and fry gently for around 10 mins until soft and slightly caramelised. Next stir in the red pepper and sweet potato, pop on the lid turning the heat to low and gently sweat the vegetables for 10 minutes.

Add the garlic, chilli, spices and salt, then cook gently for a minute or two to release the aromas, follow with the tomatoes, tomato paste, vegetable stock, beans, lime juice and syrup.

Replace the lid and gently simmer for 20 minutes until the vegetables are soft. Season generously with salt and black pepper.

Delicious served with any of the following:

1 tbsp crème fraiche or natural yogurt

A handful of fresh chopped parsley, coriander or mint

Avocado mashed with salt, lime or lemon juice

Grated pecorino or Manchego cheese

Healing visualisation

Begin by deciding to end the pain, whether it is physical pain or emotional pain. The subconscious mind rules your life. You can set your intention through the law of attraction to bring in what you want and need.

Lie down comfortably and place your left hand on your heart chakra and then your right hand on top. Gently close your eyes and focus on your heart chakra, visualising an emerald green light shining from it. Picture yourself in a place, where you have felt happy, healthy, comfortable and secure. Remember all you can about where you were; the sounds around you, sights, smells, the temperature of the air. Take in those feelings and energies of wellness and happiness again and feel them flow through your body. See yourself as you are now, healthy and happy in that place.

The body and mind do not distinguish between imagination and reality, so set your intention to feel healthy, happy and safe every day.

Awakening the mind, body and soul fruity brown rice

Affirmation

My mind is calm, my body is healthy, my soul is at peace.

Effect on the mind, body and soul

This high vibration recipe will lift your own personal vibration, which in turn will help balance you physically, mentally and spiritually. Eating whole foods with life force energy has a positive, energising effect on your physical and subtle body.

Eaten regularly, this nutritionally packed dish may help strengthen your heart, lower cholesterol, protect you from cancer and diabetes and lift your spirits, helping with any feelings of depression or anxiety.

Emotionally, the dates in the recipe provide protection from the negative energies of others; they will also help you to release any toxic emotions that may be preventing you from raising your vibration, for a more balanced you.

Preparation

Approach this recipe with love, gratitude,

appreciation and understanding of the wonderful way, in which the ingredients will contribute to healing your mind, body and soul.

Take the nuts and dried fruit in your hand, gather in their energy and in return, give your energy to these ingredients. Take time to appreciate the wonderful benefits these foods will provide; their power to awaken your soul and raise your vibration for a healthier and more balanced you.

Choose a solfeggio frequency to listen to while preparing the recipe, to raise your vibration and dispel negative energy.

Sip filtered water, with a quartz crystal in the water to ionize and remove negative energy.

Ingredients

Serves 4

250g brown basmati rice

½ tsp turmeric

1 large onion sliced

1 tbsp olive oil

Knob of butter

4 cloves garlic crushed

1 tsp ground coriander

½ tsp ground cumin

400ml organic chickpeas drained and rinsed with

filtered water

50 ml organic vegetable stock

1 tbsp chopped green olives

1 tbsp chopped raw pistachios

1 dessertspoon chopped organic dates

1 dessertspoon chopped organic apricots,

1 dessertspoon chopped organic sour cherries,

1 tbsp lemon juice

1 tbsp chopped fresh coriander

1 tbsp chopped fresh mint

1 tsp chopped fresh parsley

The Method

Cook the rice in plenty of filtered water, seasoned with the turmeric and salt. Drain and refresh with boiling water, then set aside.

Gently heat the olive oil and butter in a shallow, non-stick pan. Add the onion and cook for around 10 minutes until softened and slightly caramelised. Stir in garlic for 2-3 minutes, follow with the spices, again stirring for a couple of minutes to release their aromas. Add the chickpeas, cooked rice, olives, pistachio nuts, raisins, apricots and sour cherries, give a good stir before pouring in the vegetable stock and lemon juice. Bring to a light simmer, then cover and cook gently for 15 minutes.

Remove from the heat and carefully mix in the parsley, mint and fresh coriander.

Delicious as a light lunch or snack, served with a spoonful of yogurt and a spicy pickle or chutney.

Mindful eating

Eat this recipe mindfully, respecting the natural ingredients as you slowly chew them. To further improve your digestion, make sure that you only eat around two handfuls of the food, or only eat until you're three-quarters' full.

Meditation to awaken your soul

Try this simple meditation to raise your vibration and awaken your soul.

Sit comfortably, with your eyes closed and place your right hand on your heart chakra, then cover with your left hand. Begin visualising a blue triangle of light at the base of your spine, inhale and then exhale through this triangle, imagining shafts of light flooding down to the earth. As you inhale, visualise a cylinder of light coming up through your pelvic floor, filling and energising your entire body. Continue breathing in this way for a few minutes and then let go of the visualisation, allowing your breath to return to normal.

Setting intention

Try focusing on seeing yourself as healthy and happy. Your body acts as a puppet to your thoughts and has a tremendous capacity for self-healing. Focusing on health and not disease, provides an amazing opportunity to support well-being.

Two immune boosting cauliflower curries

Affirmation

I am calm and centred, peace surrounds me... all is well.

Effect on the mind, body and soul

These dishes are fabulous for strengthening the immune system. Cauliflower has amazing health benefits including reducing the risk of cancer, heart and brain disorders, and it even helps to relieve indigestion. This vegetable also supports eye health, detoxifies the body, and helps with weight loss too. Eaten regularly, it will also protect from the harmful effects of ultraviolet radiation, diabetes, colitis, and even hypertension!

These recipes are also calming on the nervous system. Cauliflower helps to maintain a healthy hormonal balance, which also helps to improve mood. A calm mind and body allow you to see who you truly are and reveals your own unique destiny.

Preparation

To bring peace of mind and relaxation, place at

the centre of the table, a glass bowl of *Blue Lace Agate crystals,* their beautiful periwinkle colour sends out calming and soothing vibrations.

Add next to the crystals a vase of freshly cut lavender, or place a few drops of lavender essential oil in a burner, to bring peace and serenity.

First immune boosting cauliflower curry

Ingredients

Serves 4

1 tbsp coconut oil

1 tsp cumin seeds

1tsp mustard seeds

1tsp fennel seeds

1 tbsp grated ginger

1 red chilli finely diced

1 large onion sliced

4-5 organic tomatoes chopped

2 tbsp tamarind paste

1 dessert spoon agave syrup

I medium organic cauliflower cut into small florets

400g organic chickpeas drained and rinsed

thoroughly with filtered water

2 tbsp toasted cashews roughly chopped

200ml sheep's yogurt or coconut cream

50 ml organic vegetable stock

Method

Gently heat the oil and toast the cumin, mustard and fennel seeds for a few seconds to release their aroma. Add the onion and cook for around 10 minutes until softened and lightly browned. Add the ginger and chilli and stir for a minute or two, then stir in the cauliflower for a couple of minutes before adding the chickpeas, tomatoes, tamarind paste, vegetable stock, syrup and coconut milk.

Simmer for 20 mins or until tender.

Serve with fresh coriander and coconut brown rice.

Second immune boosting cauliflower curry

Ingredients

Serves 4

1 organic cauliflower cut into florets

1 medium onion finely sliced

1 tsp cumin seeds

1 tsp mustard seeds

4 cardamom pods crushed

1 tsp turmeric powder

½ tsp chilli powder

2 tsp garam masala

4 tomatoes finely chopped

2 tbsp cashew nuts

1 tbsp pistachio nuts

2 tbsp organic raisins

2 cloves garlic crushed

2-inch piece of ginger peeled and grated

3 tbsp cream

1 tbsp coconut oil

200 ml organic vegetable stock

Fresh coriander

Method

Heat the oil and add the cumin and mustard seeds and cook until they begin to pop. Add the onion turning the heat down and cook for around 6 minutes, follow with the remaining spices, ginger, garlic and salt giving a good stir for a minute or two, you may need to add a dash of water. Stir in the cauliflower, tomatoes, nuts, raisins and vegetable stock. Cover and simmer for 10 minutes or until the cauliflower is just tender. Remove from the heat and stir in thc cream. Check the seasoning and serve with plenty of fresh coriander.

Eating with appreciation

Respect the healing ingredients in this recipe and be mindful and appreciative when eating it. Give yourself time to chew your food slowly, avoiding any tension or stress. After eating, support your digestion by lying on your left side with right hand tucked into left armpit and rest for 10-15 mins. Take the opportunity to be mindful of your affirmation, silently repeating it as you rest.

Healing to remove the pain

Make a strong intention to end the pain and to heal the body. If possible, place your hands on any area of pain and begin focusing your breath on this area. Allow every breath to be sent directly to the pain, to heal and remove it. See your breath as healing energy being directed with the clear intention of removing the pain. As you exhale, visualise this energy spreading throughout your whole body, cleansing and healing. Continue for as long as is comfortable.

To control our mind is the path to good health, inner peace and enlightenment.

Heart lifting almond and yogurt roasted whole chicken

Affirmation

My heart is healthy and strong, I'm open to giving and receiving love - I am surrounded by love.

Effect on the mind, body and soul

This easy and delicious recipe is great for supporting a healthy heart. Almonds have exceptional medicinal value and may help lower blood sugar levels, reduce blood pressure and even lower cholesterol levels. Lemon juice has remarkable healing powers and is emotionally soothing and wonderful for lifting your spirits, particularly if you've been through a difficult time.

Spiritually, this recipe teaches how to trust and open the heart to love; to trust in the flow of life, which naturally removes pressure and stress, allowing positivity in and helping a healthy heart to flourish.

Preparation

Decorate your table with white roses and emerald green crystals for love, healing, peace and balance.

Ingredients

Serves 4

1 organic or free-range chicken

Stuffing

1 lemon cut into quarters

1 cinnamon stick

3 star anise

Couple of knobs of butter

Salt and black pepper

Marinade

300 ml Greek yogurt

Juice from 2 lemons

2-inch piece of ginger, finely grated

6 garlic cloves peeled

3 shallots peeled

2 heaped tsp ground cumin,

2 heaped tsp ground coriander

1 tsp garam masala

1 tbsp blanched almonds

1 fresh green chilli

1 tsp ground fenugreek

½ tsp ground cinnamon

1 tsp coconut oil

Salt and black pepper

Dressing

100 ml of sheep's yogurt or Greek yogurt

Handful of fresh coriander finely chopped

Squeeze of fresh lemon juice

I crushed clove garlic

Salt

Cucumber pickle

1 cucumber peeled, core removed and sliced into thin matchsticks

1 tbsp sesame seeds

1 small onion finely chopped

½ tsp rock salt

2 cloves of garlic crushed

2 tbsp cider vinegar

1 tbsp coconut sugar

1 tbsp ground nut oil or grape seed oil

1 tsp rock salt

Method

Place the chicken in an ovenproof dish and stuff the chicken with the cinnamon, star anise, coriander and lemons.

Blend the marinade ingredients together excluding the yogurt, adding a dash of water to make a smooth paste, then stir in the yogurt. Make a few slits in the breast and legs of the chicken, then thoroughly coat with the marinade. If possible, leave for a few hours or even overnight.

When you are ready to cook, preheat the oven to 200°C (fan 180°C/Gas 6).

Meanwhile add a few knobs of butter to the chicken and roast in the oven for 20 mins at 200°C, then turn down the oven to 150°C degrees (fan 130C/Gas 2) for a further 2 hours, finish by roasting for a further 10 mins at 180°C (fan 160 C/Gas 4). Remove from the oven and rest for 10 minutes.

Meanwhile thoroughly mix together the yogurt dressing ingredients and set aside.

Prepare the cucumber pickle by heating the coconut oil in a small frying pan. Add the sesame seeds and cook for a minute or two or until they start to pop, immediately turn the heat down. Then add the onion and salt, cook gently for 3-5 minutes, stirring occasionally until the onion has softened. Stir in the crushed garlic, then turning the heat up slightly, stir in the cucumber and cook for a further 2-3 minutes. Stir in the vinegar and sugar, letting it bubble for a minute or two. Remove from the heat and chill before serving.

Serve with a spoonful of the yogurt dressing and the cucumber pickle

Healing meditation for the heart chakra

This only takes a few minutes and is really balancing and calming.

Lie down or sit comfortably and take a moment to feel safe, relaxed and secure in your place. Take a few breaths in and out and as you exhale, allow your eyes to close, turning your gaze softly inward and down to your heart centre. As you exhale, allow your body to release any tension or tightness that you may be holding on to.

Now focus on your heart chakra, visualise a gorgeous emerald green filling your heart space. Take a few gentle breaths here, enjoying the feeling of harmony, peace and calm that this brings. Now focus on breathing a pure white light into your heart chakra, filling this area with love and compassion. Allow yourself to rest in this shimmering white light, visualising it spreading through your entire body and radiating out to the universe and beyond, sending love, healing and positive energy to every cell.

Rest in this beautiful, healing light and when you're ready, slowly open your eyes, knowing that at any time you can come back to your healing, energising white, pure light.

Anahata Chakra

Love awakening spicy chicken with apricots and golden raisins

Affirmation

I am open to love, to receiving and giving love. I feel compassion, connection and love for others.

Effect on the mind, body and soul

This is delicious! Apricots are fantastic for rejuvenation, the fruit is loaded with over 40 trace minerals, which may help with lowering the risk of cancer and protecting DNA.

This recipe is wonderful for soothing and calming the mind, toning down any nervousness, which allows you to connect with your intuition, to discover your soul's purpose.

The apricots are energy stabilisers, so when you are feeling tired and depleted in energy, turn to this dish, as it's fabulous for bringing life back into the body.

This dish teaches you to open your heart and mind to love, to appreciate all that you have and not to take anything for granted.

Preparation

Before you begin preparing this recipe, place a rose quartz crystal in the centre of your table, to open and heal the heart. Rose is known as the stone of the heart, so fabulous for balancing the heart chakra. It helps calm emotions, releasing any negativity and bringing peace to the mind, body and soul. It's lovely to dab a drop of rose essential oil on your wrists or temples and to enjoy a beautiful vase of pink roses at your table too.

Ingredients

8 organic or free-range chicken thighs

1 tbsp organic coconut oil

2 cloves

4 green cardamom pods lightly smashed

1 fresh red chilli pricked

2-inch piece of cinnamon stick

2 star anise

1 medium onion finely sliced

4-5 large tomatoes, organic if possible, finely chopped

2-inch piece of ginger peeled and grated

4 -5 cloves garlic crushed

½ tsp chilli powder

2 tsp cumin powder

2 tsp coriander powder

1 tsp garam masala

½ tsp turmeric powder

1 tbsp coconut syrup

150g organic soft dried apricots

1 heaped tbsp organic golden raisins

2 tbsp cider vinegar

300 ml of organic vegetable stock

Salt and black pepper

A handful of fresh coriander to serve

Method

Place the chicken thighs in a shallow, oven-proof dish, sprinkle over 1 tsp of cumin and coriander powder, season with salt. Pop a knob of butter on each thigh before placing in a pre-heated oven to 200°C (fan 180°C/Gas 6) for 20 minutes or until the chicken has slightly browned. Remove and set aside.

Meanwhile, heat 1 tbsp of the oil and add the whole spices and chilli, frying for a minute or so until fragrant. Add the onion, gently frying for around 10 mins until soft and golden. Stir in the garlic, ginger, chilli powder, turmeric, garam masala, remaining cumin and coriander and a splash of water. Give a good stir and cook for a minute or two to release the flavours from the spices. Add the tomatoes and simmer for 4 to 5 minutes. Follow with the chicken giving a good stir, so that it is well coated with the spice mixture. Stir in the apricots, coconut syrup, vinegar and enough water or organic vegetable stock to just cover. Season with salt and black pepper. Bring to a gentle simmer, tightly cover the pan with a lid and pop into a preheated oven to 150 degrees (fan 130 C/Gas 2) for around one and half hours or until the chicken is tender and the sauce is a rich, thick consistency.

Serve with a handful of fresh coriander and crispy cabbage.

Crispy cabbage

1tsp black mustard seeds

1 shallot finely chopped

1 clove garlic crushed

1 cabbage finely shredded

I tbsp coconut oil

Heat the oil in a ceramic frying pan, add the seeds and when they begin to pop, add the shallot and garlic, stir for a minute or two before stirring in the cabbage. Fry for a further 5 minutes, stirring regularly until crisp and lightly golden.

Yoga sequence for opening the anahata or heart chakra

Perfect to practice either in the morning or evening on the day of cooking this recipe. This dish focuses on the heart and this sequence supports the heart chakra, the centre of love, joy and compassion. While opening your chest with these poses, focus on energetically opening your heart to love and compassion. Remind yourself of your affirmation:

I am open to love and to receiving and giving love. I feel compassion, connection and love for others.

Marjariasana - cat

The cat is a great starting posture for opening the heart. Begin on your hands and knees, keeping your shoulders above your wrists, and hips above your knees. Inhale lifting your head and tailbone towards the ceiling, then exhale arch your back, press through the shoulder blades and drop your head. Focus on bringing the shoulder blades as close together as possible on the inhale, and as far away from each other as possible on the exhale. Repeat 8 times and then move on to the next pose.

Adho mukha śvānāsana - downward facing dog

From cat, push back into downward facing dog. Press the floor away from you, as you lift your hips back and up to push yourself back into an upside-down V. Bend your knees to begin with, to lengthen the spine, then if possible, begin to straighten your legs. Rest here for as long as it's comfortable and breathe deeply, continuing to focus on the 4 counts, on your affirmation and on your heart chakra.

Bhujangasana - cobra

This pose is perfect for opening the heart chakra. Lie on your stomach and place your feet together, concentrating on pressing the tops of your feet against the floor. Place your hands underneath your shoulders, drawing your pubic bone towards the floor, to stabilize your lower back. Inhaling, lift your chest off the floor, keeping your shoulders relaxed. Hold the pose and inhale and exhale for 4 counts, focusing on the heart chakra and silently repeating the affirmation. Then on an exhalation, lower yourself back onto the ground.

Push back into child's pose and rest here for a minute or two.

Downward-Facing Dog

Bhujangasana

Soothing chicken curry, two ways

Affirmation

I love life and I am grateful for the opportunities that life offers me.

Effect on the mind, body and soul

Chicken is one of the few types of meat that is alkalising to the body, calming and soothing. These recipes are full of mood stabilizing vitamins to combat depression and anxiety, making them comforting and soothing dishes to mind and soul. They're also packed with immune boosting nutrients for a balanced and healthy body, mind and soul.

Preparation

On your table place the beautiful Gilly flower to symbolise a happy and abundant life. Then bring in the positive energy of the Peridot crystal to stimulate feelings of happiness, joy and prosperity. Now breathe in deeply and as you exhale release any tension, physical or mental that you may be holding on to. Close your eyes and take a moment to repeat the affirmation several times; giving yourself permission to be happy.

Soothing chicken curry, the first way

Ingredients

8 organic or free-range chicken thighs

1 large onion sliced

1-2 fresh green chillies

400 ml tin of organic coconut milk

200 ml of organic vegetable stock

1 tbsp ghee or coconut oil

Marinade

1 level tbsp cumin powder

1 level tbsp coriander powder

Juice from 1 lemon

Salt

Herb paste

Handful fresh coriander

2 tbsp lemon juice

A handful of fresh mint leaves

3 cloves garlic

2-inch piece ginger peeled and grated

1 tbsp pistachio nuts

1 tsp cashew nut

1 tsp fennel seeds

1 tsp ground coriander

1tsp cumin seeds

1tsp cumin powder

¼ tsp chilli powder

1 fresh green chilli

1 tsp coconut syrup or coconut sugar

Salt

Method

Rub the marinade spices into the chicken, add the salt and lemon juice and leave for a couple of hours, or overnight.

Place the chicken in an oven-proof dish, add a knob of butter to each thigh and place in a preheated oven to 200°C (fan 180°C/Gas 6) for 30 mins, until golden. Remove and set aside.

Meanwhile blend the paste ingredients to a fine puree, adding salt and enough water to make a smooth consistency.

Heat the oil in an oven proof dish, add the onion and cook until softened and golden. Add the whole chilli and stir for a minute or two, then stir in the paste for another couple of minutes, before adding the chicken, vegetable stock and coconut cream. Cover tightly with a lid and place in the oven 170 degrees (fan 150 C/Gas 3) for an hour or until tender. Delicious with coconut green beans.

Coconut green beans

Ingredients

250 g runner beans cut into 2 cm slices

1 small onion

1 green chilli

3 cloves garlic

4 tbsp organic desiccated coconut

1 tsp ground cumin

1 tsp turmeric

1 tsp mustard seeds

2 tbsp coconut oil

Method

Blend the onion, green chilli, garlic, coconut, cumin and turmeric.

In a shallow frying pan heat the oil, add the mustard seeds, as soon as they start to pop add the green beans and stir fry for 3-4 minutes. Make a hole in the centre of the beans and put in the coconut spice mixture then cover the spices with some of the beans.

Sprinkle over the salt and tbsp of filtered water. Cover with a tight-fitting lid, turn the heat to low and gently cook for around 10 minutes or until the beans have softened. The carefully stir to combine the ingredients.

Soothing chicken curry, the second way

Ingredients

1 organic chicken cut into 8 pieces

2-inch piece of ginger, peeled

3 cloves garlic

3 tbsp raw cashew nuts

3 tbsp filtered water

1 tbsp coconut oil

2 medium onions sliced

300ml natural yogurt

2 tbsp cream

2 tbsp organic raisins

5 cardamom pods lightly crushed

3-4 curry leaves

1 clove

1 stick cinnamon

2 tsp cumin seeds

½ tsp chilli powder

1 tsp garam masala

1 tsp cumin powder

1 tsp coriander powder

Juice from 1 lemon

200 ml of organic vegetable stock

Method

Place the chicken in a shallow, oven-proof dish and sprinkle over the cumin powder, coriander powder, lemon juice, salt and black pepper. If possible, leave to marinate for an hour or so and can even be left overnight. Then dot with a couple of knobs of butter and place in a pre-heated oven to 200°C (fan 180°C/Gas 6).

for 30 minutes.

Meanwhile, blend the ginger, garlic, cashews and water until you have a fine paste. Set aside.

Heat the oil and add the cardamom, curry leaves, cinnamon stick, clove and cumin seeds and stir fry for a few seconds. Add the onions and cook for around 10 minutes until softened and lightly browned. Then stir in the paste from the blender and chilli powder cooking for a further few minutes.

Remove the chicken from the oven and add it to

the mixture, with the vegetable stock and then carefully stir in the cream, yogurt, raisins and garam masala. Check the seasoning, adding a little more salt and pepper if necessary. Bring to a gentle simmer and then cover tightly and place in the oven, which has been turned down to 170 degrees (fan 150 C/Gas 3) for one hour or until the chicken is meltingly tender and the flavours have combined.

Soothing breath exercise

While the chicken is simmering, try this soothing breathing exercise, to give energy to your body, internal organs, your cells and your brain. It's so easy to do and brings a wonderful state balance and harmony to your mind, body and soul.

If possible, sit on a meditation cushion, or mat on the floor in a crossed legged mudra or in seiza, which is a Japanese meditation kneeling position. If this is difficult then sit comfortably upright on a chair. Place the crystal Mookaite Jasper on the floor in front of you.

Bring hands together in prayer position, in front of your chest and a little higher than your heart. The tops of the middle fingers, representing the fire element, should meet. Visualise breathing in energy or light flowing into your hands, moving along your arms, down through your body into your Hara. Then breathe out, imagining the energy from your Hara flowing through your body, arms and out through your hands, before spreading in all directions across the world and the Universe.

Focus on where your middle fingers touch and try to release stray thoughts by focusing on this point and even press the two middle fingers against each other to help to focus. Continue for a few minutes.

Ancient healing chickpea burgers

Affirmation

My body knows how to heal itself, being healthy is my natural state.

Effect on the mind, body and soul

Chickpeas are one of the oldest consumed crops in the world and have so many wonderful nutritional benefits. They have been used since ancient times for healing, from lowering inflammation, preventing diabetes, improving the heart and digestion and boosting the health of the eyes and skin. They are also a natural way to balance hormones, making this dish perfect to eat to improve feelings of happiness and wellbeing.

Preparation

While you are preparing the ingredients, try sipping some filtered water with 1 tbsp raw, organic cider vinegar added to it; this is great for weight loss as it prevents you from over eating and helps with the digestion of the burgers.

Ingredients

Makes 8 burgers

1 large onion finely chopped

1 medium organic carrot grated

2 cloves garlic

1 tsp ground cumin

1 tsp ground coriander

1 tsp garam masala

Pinch of red chilli powder

Handful fresh coriander finely chopped

2 tbsp lemon or lime juice

400g tin of organic chickpeas, rinsed and drained

1 tbsp chopped pumpkin seeds

2 heaped tsp tahini paste

2 tbsp olive oil

Salt

Method

Heat 1 tbsp of oil and gently soften the onion for 8-10 minutes, until slightly caramelised. Then stir in the carrot and garlic and cook gently for another 5 minutes until slightly softened. Add the spices with a splash of water and cook for a minute or two before stirring in the chickpeas. Season generously with salt and black pepper.

Pop on the lid and turn the heat down and let the mixture sweat and soften for around 5 minutes. Keep an eye on it, occasionally stirring and if necessary, add a splash of water.

Remove from the heat and stir in the fresh coriander, seeds, lemon juice and tahini. Check the seasoning and briefly pulse about two thirds of the mixture with a food processor or blender, so that the mixture is well combined but still has some texture. Then give a good stir, check the seasoning and if the mixture is a little dry add a dash more lemon juice. Add the remaining third and shape into medium sized patties. Place in the fridge to chill for at least an hour or until you are ready to cook them.

Heat the remaining olive oil in a frying pan and cook the patties on both sides for a few minutes, or until they are golden brown. Place them in a preheated oven to 180 degrees for 5 minutes or until they have warmed through.

Serve with fresh tomato, spring onion and coriander salsa, crisp green salad with a lemony vinaigrette and yogurt and feta dressing.

To support the healing qualities of this meal and to aid in its digestion, follow with

Digestion strengthening baked pears

Ingredients

8 large organic pears, peeled and cored

1 tbsp maple syrup

1 stick of cinnamon

2 star anise

1-inch root ginger sliced

200 ml organic apple juice

100 ml freshly squeezed orange juice

Zest from 1 orange

1 tbsp walnuts roughly chopped

1 tbsp organic dates roughly chopped

Place the pears upright in a tight-fitting saucepan and cover with the apple and orange juice. Then add the syrup, cinnamon, star anise, ginger, dates and orange zest. Bring to a gentle simmer, cover and cook for around one hour or until the pears are soft and tender. Remove from the heat, scatter over the walnuts and serve with a spoonful of crème fraiche.

Healing and balancing body oil

Fabulous for improving skin elasticity, smoothing and toning the body. Organic and natural, using oils including Frankincense, Rose and Geranium, which heal and balance not only the body but the mind and soul too.

Jojoba oil 20ml

Pomegranate seed oil 5ml

Vitamin E oil 5ml

Argan oil 20ml

6 drops Frankincense

5 drops Rose

4 drops Juniper

3 drops Rosemary

3 drops Neroli

4 drops Geranium

Mix all the ingredients and store in a sterilised glass bottle.

Repeat the affirmation as you enjoy massaging this healing oil into your skin; perfect to use after a warm bath or shower.

Gut protecting miso marinated cod with miso pickle

Affirmation

I lovingly forgive myself and others. I choose to fill my world with love and joy.

Effect on the mind, body and soul

"It isn't what you eat that ages you. It's what happens to what you eat that ages you."

This recipe is protective and supportive to the gut. You need to heal the gut so that food's vital lifegiving attributes have the best possible chance to get through and do their work. Protecting the gut is so important to improving your health and vitality. Your gut is your second brain, it reacts to all your feelings, thoughts, desires and fears and any stress or negative thoughts immediately upset the balance and health of the gut, which in turn upsets the balance and health of the entire body. Spiritually the carrots in this pickle represent fertility, growth and the ability to see clearly.

Preparation

For a cooling, digestive boost, calmly prepare this recipe sipping a glass of filtered water mixed with a pinch of dry ginger, ground fennel seeds, cumin powder and a slice of lemon or lime.

Ingredients

Marinade

4 cod loins from sustainable sources

2 tbsp brown rice miso paste

4 tbsp cooking sake

2 tbsp mirin

1 tbsp brown rice vinegar

1 tbsp sesame oil

1 tbsp sesame seeds

1 tbsp coconut oil

Juice from 1 lime

Miso pickle

1 tbsp brown rice miso

2 tbsp brown rice vinegar

1 tbsp coconut sugar or syrup

1 garlic clove crushed

400g organic carrots finely sliced into slim batons

The Method

Start by making the miso pickle: put the miso, vinegar, coconut sugar or syrup and half teaspoon salt in a bowl, add the garlic and carrots and stir well. Cover the bowl and leave to pickle in the fridge for 24 hours (this will keep in a jar for up to 1 month).

The day before eating, thoroughly whisk the marinade ingredients together, pat the cod fillets completely dry with paper towels. Coat the fish with the miso marinade and place in a glass dish and cover tightly. Leave to marinate for a few hours or overnight.

When you're ready to cook, preheat oven to 180 degrees (fan 160 C/Gas 4). Meanwhile heat a little coconut oil in a shallow frying pan, place the fish skin-side-up in the pan and cook only for a minute or two until the bottom of the fish browns and blackens in spots, turn the fish over doing the same on the other side. Transfer to the oven and bake for 5 to 10 minutes, until fish is cooked. Scatter over the toasted sesame seeds.

Serve with the carrot pickle, shredded spinach or watercress, lime wedges and fresh coriander

Detox night routine

On the evening of eating this recipe, stimulate your lymphatic system by dry skin brushing. This will help release toxins, encourage the elimination of metabolic waste and support your digestion. Your skin will glow and feel tighter!

Follow with a warm bath of Epsom salts, which will further flush the toxins and any heavy metals from your cells, easing muscle pain and helping the body to eliminate harmful substances. Mix 5 drops of lavender oil, 3 drops juniper oil and 3 drops of bergamot in a tablespoon of almond oil and then add to your bath water along with a couple of good handfuls of Epsom salts.

A beautiful way to relax and detox before bed!

Heart-warming fish pie

Affirmation

My heart is open to receiving and giving love. I'm grateful and appreciate all that I have!

Effect on the mind, body and soul

This is a perfect dish to enjoy with family and friends; it is so comforting and heart-warming. Fish is a fabulous superfood, being a major source of omega-3 fatty acids and packed with vitamins and minerals. It will help to protect your body against diseases, such as cancer, heart disease and arthritis. It also has a positive effect on the mind, strengthening your nervous system and protecting against depression.

Preparation

In your kitchen, place a drop of geranium, frankincense, orange and bergamot in a diffuser to inspire gratitude, appreciation and love. Sit comfortably, closing your eyes and breathing deeply for a couple of minutes; with each breath focus on all that you are grateful for. Decide to spend the rest of the day being mindful of appreciation and gratitude, rather than expectation.

Ingredients

Serves 4-6

200 g skinless, boneless white fish, such as hake, haddock, cod, from sustainable sources

200 g skinless boneless salmon, from sustainable sources

200 g skinless, boneless undyed smoked haddock, from sustainable sources

1 kg floury organic potatoes peeled

2-3 knobs of butter

1 tbsp olive oil

50 g pecorino cheese finely grated

6-7 shallots peeled and finely diced

2 leeks peeled and finely sliced

50 ml white wine or organic vegetable stock

1 tsp Dijon mustard

300 ml organic crème fraîche

2 tbsp chopped fresh parsley

2 handfuls fresh spinach roughly chopped

2 tbsp lemon juice

1 tbsp capers finely chopped

Salt and black pepper

Method

Preheat the oven to 200°C (fan 180°C/Gas 6).

Make the topping by boiling the potatoes in a pan of salted water for 15-20 minutes, or until tender. Drain and mash with the butter and 50 ml of the crème fraiche, season with salt and pepper and set aside.

Meanwhile, gently heat the olive oil and a knob of butter, add the shallots and gently cook without burning until softened. Stir in the leeks, add a splash of water, pop on a lid and cook on low heat for 5 minutes or until the leeks have softened. Add the wine letting it bubble for a minute or two before stirring in the lemon juice, capers, mustard, parsley, crème fraiche and season with salt and pepper.

Carefully place the fish in the sauce, replace the lid and simmer gently for 5 minutes. Remove from the heat, add the chopped spinach and tip into your baking dish. Spoon over the mash potatoes and top with the grated cheese and a few knobs of butter.

Bake in the oven for 30-40 minutes, or until the pie is bubbling around the edges and piping hot in the centre.

Energy boosting coconut and date treats

These are easy, quick and tasty and wonderful for a sweet energy boost at any time throughout the day.

Ingredients

2tbsp organic dates

1 tbsp desiccated organic coconut

1 tbsp pumpkin seeds

1 tbsp blanched almonds

1 tbsp raw cashew nuts

1 tbsp organic dried apricots

Juice from half an orange

Extra desiccated coconut for dusting

Method

Blend the ingredients, roll into small balls and dust with additional desiccated coconut. Delicious with your favourite herbal or fruit tea!

Relaxing and heart opening yoga pose

After eating, try this relaxing pose to open your heart chakra.

Lie down and position a bolster, blanket roll, or

yoga block under your upper back and head. Allow yourself to soften into the support. Close your eyes and relax your arms beside you with palms turned up. Focus on your heart chakra, visualising a beautiful emerald green ball of energy, then silently repeat the affirmation, allowing it to inspire feelings of love and gratitude in your heart.

Confidence boosting harissa lamb with chickpeas and dates

Affirmation

I deserve to be happy and successful. I am confident and can achieve all that I desire.

Effect on the mind, body and soul

This is delicious and so nutritious. Dates have massive health benefits from preventing cancer, strengthening the digestive system, improving bone health and boosting energy. Eating this dish regularly will improve your mood, give you more energy, help you think more clearly and improve your self-esteem for a more confident you.

Preparation

Take a moment to centre yourself and repeat the affirmation 12 times; feel the warm glow of confidence and success fill your mind, body and soul. Approach this recipe with detached attachment.

"Your heart must become a sea of love. Your mind must become a river of detachment."

- Sri Chinmoy

Ingredients

750g lamb trimmed and cut into pieces

2 tbsp olive oil

2-inch piece fresh root ginger, finely grated

3 cloves garlic peeled and crushed

1 fresh red chilli finely chopped

2 red onions, thinly sliced

2 tsp ground cumin

2 tsp ground coriander

200ml dry white wine

400g tin organic chopped tomatoes

1 tbsp sundried tomato purée

1 tbsp clear raw honey

1 tbsp rose harissa paste

1 lime, juice and finely grated rind

6-7 organic dates chopped

400g tin organic chick peas drained and rinsed

200ml fresh chicken stock or organic vegetable stock

Salt and freshly ground black pepper

A handful of fresh coriander

Method

Brown the meat on all sides in 1 tbsp of olive oil.

Remove and add the sliced onions, cook gently for 10 mins until softened and lightly browned.

Next stir in the ginger, garlic, fresh chilli, cumin, coriander and cook gently for a minute or two stirring constantly. Pour in the wine and simmer for 5 mins until it has slightly reduced. Stir in the harissa paste, honey, tomatoes, sundried tomato paste, dates, lime juice and rind, finishing with the fresh chicken or vegetable stock. Add the lamb, chickpeas and season with salt and pepper.

Bring to the boil and place in a preheated oven to 170 degrees (fan 150 C/Gas 3) and cook gently for one and half hours or until the meat is meltingly tender.

Accompany with a dish of crumbled feta mixed with freshly chopped coriander, a squeeze of lemon juice, chopped fresh red chilli and a drizzle olive oil.

Serve with a salad of spinach, watercress, avocado, roasted red pepper and pine nuts

This recipe is equally good as a vegetarian dish by omitting the meat and using a mix of chickpea and cannellini beans.

Mindful breathing for confidence

Try this mindful breathing exercise, which helps you remain focused in the present by activating your solar plexus chakra, located in your abdomen, above your belly button. This subtle energy centre connects you to an inner state of confidence and self-esteem.

The technique is simple, you simply focus on your breath.

Sit comfortably, placing your hands on your solar plexus, right hand lying on top of the left. Close your eyes and bring your attention to your solar plexus, and begin focusing on your breath, try not to force anything, just allow the breath to take place, appreciating its wonder. As you inhale visualise a bright warm golden ball of light in your solar plexus, hold that energy ball of light there for a moment or two and then as you exhale let that light radiate out from your whole body and into the universe. Continue for as long as is comfortable and if your mind wanders, then gently bring it back to the breath flowing in through your nostrils and out through your entire body.

"Feelings come and go like clouds in a windy sky. Conscious breathing is my anchor."

- Thich Nhat Hanh, Stepping into Freedom

Optimism and contentment boosting spiced lamb with sour cherries

Affirmation

I see the good in everything and feel hopeful, light hearted and content.

Effect on the mind, body and soul

This delicious recipe will improve any feelings of negativity or unhappiness. The cherries will help you to feel more hopeful and optimistic, to see the good in everything. Cherries contain melatonin, a hormone to balance sleep patterns, so eating this dish will have a restoring effect on your body, helping you get a better night's sleep. They can also lower cholesterol, improve your immune system, and keep you feeling youthful and invigorated!

Preparation

Place a beautiful citrine crystal for hope and cheerfulness at the centre of the table. Remember to wash your crystal first in filtered water, drying it in direct sunlight to re-energise it. Hold the crystal for a moment or two and allow yourself a couple of minutes to sit quietly, releasing any worries or criticisms that you may be holding onto, knowing that by doing so will lead to feelings of contentment and emotionally stability. Finish by replacing the crystal at the centre of your table, alongside a vase of yellow daffodils, tulips or roses.

Ingredients

700 g leg of lamb trimmed and cut into small pieces

2 medium onions sliced

5 green cardamom pods lightly smashed

3/4 curry leaves

2 tsp cumin powder

2 tsp coriander powder

2 tbsp coconut oil

1tsp cumin seeds

2 inches ginger peeled and grated

4 cloves garlic peeled and crushed

2-3 red chillies cut lengthwise and seeds removed

225 ml homemade chicken or vegetable stock

350 ml Greek style natural yogurt

25g fresh coriander chopped

70g dried cherries, organic if possible

Salt and black pepper

Method

Sprinkle the salt, cumin and coriander powder over lamb and massage in the spices, then marinate for at least 45 mins (even better overnight)

Heat coconut oil and fry in batches on high heat until browned all over. Remove the meat from the pan.

Meanwhile, heat 1 tbsp of coconut oil and stir in the cumin seeds, cardamom and curry leaves for a minute or until they just begin to pop, immediately add the onion giving a good stir, turn the heat down to allow the onions to gently cook until softened and lightly browned.

Stir in the ginger, garlic, chilli, cherries, 1 tsp cumin powder, 1 tsp coriander powder and salt and black pepper. Give a good stir for a minute or two to soften and combine, then add the stock and carefully stir in the yogurt, finish with the coriander. Check the seasoning and if you'd like a little more heat add ¼ tsp chilli powder.

Cover tightly and place in a preheated oven to 170 degrees (fan 150 C/Gas 3) for one and half hours or until tender.

Serve with plenty of fresh coriander and a

spoonful of yogurt.

Roasted cauliflower with spinach and yogurt

Ingredients

I head of organic cauliflower cut into florets (approx. 1-2 inches each)

A couple of handfuls of fresh spinach

Juice of 1 lemon

Marinade

225 ml natural organic yogurt

4 cloves garlic crushed

1 tbsp fresh ginger grated

Juice and zest from half lemon

2 tsp tamarind paste.

Handful fresh coriander

Pistachio nuts roughly chopped

Method

Combine the marinade ingredients in a bowl, then add the cauliflower florets. Stir to thoroughly coat the cauliflower and leave to marinade in the fridge for around 3 - 4 hours (can be left overnight).

Preheat the oven to 170 degrees (fan 150 C/Gas 3). Place the cauliflower in a shallow casserole dish, add a few knobs of butter and roast for around 45 mins or until tender.

Remove from the oven and fold in the spinach, allowing the heat to lightly soften it.

Squeeze over the lemon juice, sprinkle over the pistachio nuts, chopped coriander and a spoonful of yogurt.

5 Minute visualisation for happiness

Perfect to enjoy after eating this recipe

Sit comfortably and close your eyes. Take a moment to mentally relax your body, begin with focusing on your feet, then travel up your legs, your back, belly, fingers, hands, arms, shoulders, neck and then soften all the muscles in your face. Take a big breath into your belly and exhale fully, releasing any tension. Now imagine yourself sitting in the middle of a cherry tree orchard, right in the middle of this orchard is the biggest tree ripe with cherries. See yourself picking the red ripe fruit and feeling light-hearted, happy and carefree as you do so. As you enjoy picking and eating the sweet ripe fruit, allow any problems and worries to easily and quickly dissolve away. Now as you walk away from the cherry orchard, feel that your cares and worries have lifted, feel hope and optimism spread like a warm glow through your whole body. When you are ready, open eyes with a feeling of optimism and balance of spirit, body and mind.

Detoxifying and healing coconut cream mung bean daal

Affirmation

I trust in the natural rhythm and flow of life and I release my body from any negative energy or thoughts.

Effect on the mind, body and soul

This tasty daal is fantastic for strengthening the gut and improving digestion, which is helpful with improving your overall health.

It is packed with nutritional benefits and a must to eat regularly. Ginger is a wonderful nerve tonic, helping to relieve stress, release tension and calm the mind, and the fresh turmeric deals with any inflammation in the body that's causing pain. This recipe is also great for the cardiovascular system, lowering bad cholesterol and helping to prevent cancer. The combined ingredients in this daal even help to extract toxic heavy metals from your body.

This daal teaches you to let go of negative situations that block your natural flow of energy. When you don't have answers, rather than feeling the need to react, you understand the spiritual benefit of letting go.

It suits all body types and is especially great to eat in the spring, a time for detoxifying.

Preparation

Prepare this recipe mindfully, understanding that the ingredients are all there to provide you with the nutrients and energy for healing and balancing your mind, body and soul, so prepare with gratitude and appreciation.

Try listening to a solfreggio frequency for cleansing negative energy and thought pattern, as you mindfully eat this daal, making sure that you eat slowly and thoughtfully. Burning sandalwood incense stick and setting the table with a beautifully pure Quartz crystal, will soak up any negative energies.

Ingredients

Serves 4

350 g mung beans

1 tbsp coconut oil

2 – 3 curry leaves

6 cm piece of cinnamon stick

1 tsp black mustard seeds

1 large onion sliced

3 large cloves of garlic

6 cm fresh ginger

1 cm fresh turmeric root, peeled and grated

1 fresh red chilli finely sliced

1 tsp ground coriander

1 tsp ground cumin

1 tsp garam masala

100ml organic coconut milk

300g of fresh tomatoes finely chopped

1 tbsp lime juice

1 tbsp coconut syrup

Method

Wash the beans in plenty of cold water, then cover with fresh cold water and leave to soak overnight. The next day, put the beans into a large pan and cover with fresh water. Bring to a simmer, cover the pan with a lid and cook on low heat for 10 mins or until the lentils are completely tender. Drain and set aside.

Meanwhile, heat the oil in a frying pan over medium heat, add the curry leaves, cinnamon stick and black mustard seeds. Fry for 1 minute until fragrant, then add the onion and fry for 10 mins until golden. Meanwhile make a paste with the ginger, garlic, turmeric and chilli (either use a blender or finely chop or pestle and mortar).

Then add the paste and spices, stirring for a minute or two before adding the chopped tomatoes, coconut milk, coconut syrup, salt and lemon juice. Cover and simmer for 10 mins. Stir in the cooked mung beans and simmer for a further15 mins.

Serve plenty of chopped fresh coriander, brown rice and spiced roasted cauliflower.

Natural cleansing body scrub

"The body is your temple. Keep it pure and clean for the soul to reside in."

- B.K.S. Iyengar

This detoxifying scrub is perfect to use in the morning before eating this daal, as it will beautifully support its detoxifying effect.

Ingredients

1 tbsp olive oil

1 tbsp shea butter

5 tbsp dead sea salt

3 drops lemon oil

5 drops lavender oil

4 drops rosemary oil

Method

Mix the ingredients together thoroughly and leave to combine for around 10 minutes. Gently massage the scrub onto dry skin, leaving it on for a few minutes, before washing off with warm water.

Powerful ancient cleansing breath

Follow with Kapalabhati, a powerful cleansing yogic breath to release the toxins and energise the body.

Kapalabhati consists of a steady repetition of forceful exhalations, followed by slightly slower, passive inhalations. Exhalations are generated by powerful contractions of the lower belly which push air out of the lungs. Inhalations are responses to the release of this contraction, which sucks air back into the lungs.

Sit comfortably, preferably cross-legged if possible, rest your hands on your knees, close your eyes and turn your attention to your lower belly. Take a deep breath in and exhale fully, then breath in and quickly contract your lower belly, pushing a burst of air out of your lungs. Then quickly release the contraction, so the belly "rebounds" to suck air into your lungs. Pace yourself slowly at first, repeating 20 to 25 times. Finish by exhaling fully, then take a big breath in and out, then breathe in and hold the breath for around 5 or 6 counts before exhaling.

Vibration raising sesame noodles

Affirmation

My mind and body are energised and nourished. I feel great! I am healthy and happy.

Effect on the mind, body and soul

This is a great pick-me-up when you want to boost your wellbeing, it will leave you feeling nourished and energised. The seeds are superb mood lift lifters, helping to balance your emotions, to leave you feeling positive and centred. Asparagus, known as the fountain of youth, along with the other vegetables, is wonderful for lifting your vibration and balancing your health.

Preparation

Prepare this recipe with the appreciation of love; the love for yourself, your family, friends, animals and love of the universe. Focus on the energy of the tarot card, the Ten of Cups, which embraces love and embodies happiness and contentment. Choose any pink or green crystal to place on your table to bring more love into your life. Make a conscious decision to invest in organic vegetables, to reinforce the life force energy of this dish.

TEN OF CUPS

Ingredients

200 g spelt noodles cooked and drained

1 tbsp sesame seeds

1 tbsp sunflower seeds

1 tbsp pumpkin seeds

Dressing

2 tbsp sesame oil

1 tbsp walnut oil

1 tbsp brown rice vinegar

2 tbsp tamari

2 tbsp sweet chilli sauce

2 tbsp lime juice

1 tsp cashew nut butter

1 clove crushed garlic

Salad

Fresh coriander finely chopped

1 tbsp mangetout sliced in half lengthways

1 tbsp small broccoli florets lightly steamed

1 handful asparagus tips thinly sliced lengthways, lightly steamed

Baby corn thinly sliced long ways

Handful of fresh beansprouts

1 red pepper cut into long strips

1 yellow pepper cut into long strips

2-3 spring onions finely sliced

Method

Toast the seeds in a dry pan over medium heat for 5 minutes, stirring occasionally, until they just begin to brown. This releases their natural flavour.

Whisk dressing, then assemble the salad, toss in the noodles and then thoroughly combine with the dressing. Finely sprinkle with the sunflower and sesame seeds and fresh coriander.

Cleansing room mist

Beautiful for lifting the vibration and cleansing any negative energy throughout your home.

100ml spring water

5 drops frankincense

3 drops lavender

3 drops cypress

2 drops peppermint

3 drops sage

Fill a sterilised, glass spray bottle with the spring

water, add the oils giving a good shake to thoroughly mix. Spray your rooms regularly, repeating the affirmation:

I love myself and I am surrounded by love

to lift the vibration and remove any negative energy.

Cleansing aura practice

This energising and relaxing practice is also wonderful for cleansing your aura and lifting your vibration.

Find a warm and comfortable place to lie down on your back. Place your legs hip- distance apart and allow your feet to flop out. Place your arms shoulder-width from the body, turning palms up.

Close your eyes and take a couple of slow, deep breaths through the nose. Allow your whole body to become soft and heavy with each exhalation; feel completely supported by the floor that you're lying on. Scan the body from the toes to the fingers, to the crown of the head, consciously releasing any tension and tightness and allowing your body to move into a deeper and deeper state of relaxation.

Now bring your attention to your breath, inhale

deeply bringing the breath into your hara, the area just below your navel, hold the breath here for 4 counts then exhale through your skin, through to your aura and to the universe and beyond. Repeat several times and then let your breath go and quietly repeat your affirmation. Then release all thought and enjoy the stillness of your body and mind for as long as you feel comfortable.

Gut soothing potato salad

Affirmation

I approach my life in harmony, living peacefully, with calmness and self-control.

Effect on the mind, body and soul

This is a superfood healing recipe; seeds are one of nature's most potent foods, supporting your good health. It is soothing, energy restoring and will help lead you to balance and harmony in the way you lead your life.

Preparation

Connecting to your inner peace requires allowing moments of silence. Making time to remove yourself from stimulating activities will re-energise your body and remove any anxiety and tensions from your mind. Take a moment before preparing this recipe to sit quietly and silently repeat the affirmation. Then as you prepare the ingredients, do so mindfully and with a quiet awareness of their healing energies.

Ingredients

450g organic baby potatoes peeled and cut in half

1 tbsp hemp seeds

1 tbsp pumpkin seeds

1 tbsp sunflower seeds

1 tbsp capers chopped

1 tbsp gherkins finely chopped

Handful fresh herbs, chives, mint, parsley, dill finely chopped

90g wild rocket

1 tbsp tahini paste

2 tbsp lemon juice

3 tbsp olive oil

2 tsp agave syrup

Salt and black pepper

Method

Boil the potatoes in lightly salted water with a couple of sprigs of mint, for 10 minutes or until the potatoes have cooked. Drain and remove the mint sprigs.

In a small frying pan, lightly toast the pumpkin, sunflower and hemp seeds, stirring frequently for a minute or two until they just begin to brown slightly. Then pop them into a pestle and mortar and roughly crush.

Whisk the olive oil, tahini, lemon juice and agave

syrup and season with salt and pepper. You may need to add a dash of filtered water if the dressing is a little thick. Pour the dressing over the warm potatoes giving a good stir. Then fold in the gherkin, capers and fresh herbs, check the seasoning adding an extra squeeze of lemon juice if necessary. Finish by scattering over the crushed seeds.

Delicious served on a bed of fresh rocket leaves, drizzled with lemony garlic oil.

Breathing practice for soothing the mind, body and spirit

"Breath is the king of mind."

- B.K.S. Iyengar

This powerful yoga breathing exercise is so effective in relieving stress and anxiety, bringing calm and stillness to the mind and body. It's even effective in reducing high blood pressure and a must for those who have trouble sleeping!

- Sit in any comfortable seated position, relax the body and breathe naturally for a few moments, allowing your mind and body to settle.

- Rest your left hand on your lap or knee and fold the index and middle finger toward the palm. Place your thumb gently onto your right nostril and place your ring and little fingers gently onto your left nostril.
- Close your eyes and begin by closing your right nostril (using your right thumb) and inhale smoothly, gently and without strain through your left nostril.
- Close your left nostril (using your ring and little fingers) and release closure of your right. Exhale through your right nostril. Inhale through your right nostril. Close your right nostril and release closure of your left. Exhale through your left nostril.
- This completes one round. Continue this pattern for as long as you are comfortable, I suggest aiming to complete at least 5 rounds. When you're finished relax both arms, sit and breathe naturally for a few moments before opening your eyes.

Namaste

I honour the place in you
In which the entire Universe dwells
I honour the place in you
Which is of love, of truth, of light and of peace
When you are in that place in you
And I am in that place in me
We are one

Flexibility and youth boosting thai pork curry

Affirmation

I am grateful for a youthful and flexible mind, body and spirit. I accept the flow of life.

Effect on the mind, body and soul

This is a wonderful dish for keeping you flexible and agile, as turmeric is great for reducing inflammation to help relieve arthritis and joint pain. A flexible body ensures a flexible mind and attitude to life, which is fundamental in a healthy balanced mind, body and soul. The nuts here are packed with health benefits to keep your body strong and healthy.

Preparation

Prepare this recipe with the awareness of gratitude. Start writing a gratitude diary and take a moment to list all the things that you appreciate in your life. Now turn your attention to these ingredients, take them in your hands and thank the universe for their healing energies.

Place the 9 of Cups tarot card on your table and contemplate the message of this card; to count your blessings. Live in the moment and be grateful for the good things that life has to offer you. Practised regularly, you will find that your feelings of contentment and fulfilment will increase.

Ingredients

1 kg shoulder of pork cut into 2-inch cubes

4 lime leaves

1 tin organic coconut cream

Juice from 1 lime

2 medium onions, finely sliced

1 tbsp tamari

1 tsp fish sauce

2 tbsp coconut oil

20 ml of organic vegetable stock

1 tbsp cashew nuts

Paste

20g fresh ginger peeled and grated

15 g fresh turmeric peeled and grated

6 shallots peeled and roughly chopped

6 large cloves garlic peeled and roughly chopped

2 fresh red chillies finely chopped

I tbsp of raw cashew nuts

1 tbsp blanched almonds

2 tsp coconut sugar

Juice from 1 lime

Zest from 1 lime

1 lemongrass stick soaked in water for an hour or so and sliced

A handful fresh coriander

Salt and black pepper

1 tbsp water

Method

Preheat the oven to 170 degrees (fan 150 C/Gas 3)

To make the paste, place all the ingredients in a blender, with a dash of water and blend to a smooth paste.

Meanwhile, heat the oil and brown the meat over high heat, remove and set aside.

Add a little more coconut oil if needed, then throw in the lime leaves for a minute or so, followed by the onion and cook for around 10 minutes on low heat or until onion begins to caramelise.

Stir in the paste, cook for a couple of minutes then stir in the meat and thoroughly coat in the paste. Add the coconut cream, vegetable stock, tamari, lime juice, zest and fish sauce. Bring to a gentle simmer, then pop on the lid and place in the oven for 2 hours until the pork is tender, and the flavours have combined.

Toast a tablespoon of cashew nuts and scatter over the pork, along with a handful of fresh coriander. Delicious served with coconut rice.

Yoga pose for gratitude

Seated Forward Fold – Paschimottanasana

This wonderful pose inspires gratitude as your attention is focused inwards.

Come to a comfortable seated position, extending your legs in front of you. (You may find it more comfortable to prop yourself up on a pillow or blanket.)
Reach your arms up as you inhale and fold forward over your legs as you exhale. As you breathe calmly, consider one part of your body for which you are especially grateful.

Mood lifting pea, watercress and leek soup

Affirmation

I release the need to replay situations in my mind and I transform all negative energy into love and light... I welcome health and happiness.

Effect on the mind, body and soul

Make this soup to lift your mood and to nurture your mind, body and soul. It's nutritionally packed and should leave you feeling calm, contented and nurtured. It will help to protect you from breast cancer, strengthen your heart, your bones, your thyroid, your eyes and it's packed with vitamin C to help ward off colds.

Preparation

Place a rose quartz crystal in the kitchen for its healing and nurturing nature. Then before you begin preparing this recipe, practise Kenyoku Ho, which means "dry brushing" and is a simple effective way to remove any negative energy.

Sit comfortably, preferably in a kneeling position if possible, and place the fingertips of your right hand near the top of your left shoulder, with your hand flat, take a deep breath in and exhale forcefully with a “haa” sound simultaneously drawing your hand down and across your chest in a straight line to the right hip. Do the same on the right side and then repeat just once more on the left side.

Now, with your left arm horizontal to the floor, place your right hand on the left forearm and move it flat in a sweeping movement all the way to the fingertips (and beyond) exhaling “haa” as you do so. Repeat on the right side and then again on the left side.

Ingredients

1 onion roughly chopped

2 leeks sliced

2 cloves garlic chopped

1 medium organic potato peeled and cut into cubes

100g watercress

400g peas

1 litre organic vegetable stock made with filtered water

1 tbsp olive oil

Knob of butter

Salt and black pepper

1 tbsp double cream or crème fraiche

Method

Gently heat the butter and oil, then stir in the onion, garlic, leek, potato, salt and pepper and a splash of the stock. Pop on the lid turning the heat to low and gently steam the vegetables for around 20 minutes or until soft.

Stir in the watercress and gently steam for 3 minutes, add the peas and vegetable stock. Bring to a gently simmer for just a minute and then remove from the heat.

Puree until smooth and carefully stir in the cream.

Garnish with a spoonful of nurturing pea pesto, a few extra toasted pine nuts, shredded basil or mint leaves and a spoonful of natural yogurt or crème fraiche.

Nurturing pea pesto

Make this quick and easy pesto to lift your mood and to nurture your mind, body and soul. It's nutritionally packed and will leave you feeling calm, contented and nurtured.

Ingredients

200g peas

Handful fresh basil

A handful of fresh mint

2 tbsp of pine nuts

1 small clove of garlic

1 tbsp of capers

1 tbsp of green olives* optional

1 tbsp grated Wensleydale or Pecorino cheese grated *optional

Salt and black pepper

1 tbsp olive oil

A squeeze of lime juice, a drizzle of olive oil and extra pine nuts to serve

Method

So simple but so tasty, all you need to do is blend together all the ingredients until you have a chunky paste, spoon into a bowl and drizzle with a little extra olive oil, squeeze of lime and a scattering of pine nuts

This is also great on some griddled, homemade spelt bread, stirred into pasta, brown rice or with roasted vegetables, garlic roasted chicken, grilled fish or even great with a jacket potato or as a quick topping for your toast!

Meditation to lift your mood

After eating, enjoy this cleansing and mind focusing meditation.

Sit comfortably, closing your eyes, keeping your gaze soft and focused on your heart chakra. Bring your hands together in prayer position, in front of your chest and a little higher than your heart. Begin visualising breathing in energy, which you see as a bright white light, flowing through your fingers, moving along your arms, down your body into your Hara. Then breath out, imagining the energy from your Hara flowing through your body, then your arms and then out through your hands, before spreading in all directions across the world and the universe. Focus on where your middle fingers touch and try to release stray thoughts by bringing your attention back to this point and even press the two middle fingers against each other to help keep the focus, continue breathing in this way for a few minutes. Then relax the breath, keeping your eyes closed and enjoying the peace and calm in your mind, body and soul.

Physical and spiritual energy raising roasted quinoa salad

Affirmation

I can see clearly my soul purpose. I have been given all the gifts to achieve all that I want to achieve. I feel strong, confident and safe.

Effect on the mind, body and soul

Quinoa is literally a wonder food! An ancient grain cultivated in South America, it was called the "gold of the Incas" because it increased the strength and stamina of their warriors. It's gluten free, a complete protein, high in fibre and packed with B-vitamins, iron, potassium, calcium, phosphorus, vitamin E and antioxidants. It's fantastic for healing; it can strengthen your bones, help prevent cancer, heart disease, diabetes and even help you lose weight.

Eating this recipe regularly will help your body's energy vibration to rise, enhancing your spiritual energy, enabling you to overcome your life's problems and challenges and help you see clearly your unique universal purpose.

Preparation

Begin by raising the vibration of your kitchen and

dining room by cleansing the room. It's important to first declutter and thoroughly clean the room, then smudge all four corners with sage or an incense stick. Take a singing bowl and strike it, particularly in the areas where you feel that the energy has stagnated. Light a candle and play a solfreggio frequency for removing negative energies.

Wash a large selenite crystal in cold water, placing it in the sun to dry and energise. Then place at the centre of your table to raise the room's vibration and to protect it from negative energy.

Ingredients

75 g quinoa

2 tbsp extra virgin olive oil

2 medium sweet potatoes peeled and cut into cubes

1 carrot peeled and cut into small cubes

1 red pepper diced

1 red onion peeled and cut into large dice

¼ tsp red chilli powder

1 tsp cumin powder

2 tbsp pumpkin seeds

1 tbsp dried organic cranberries soaked in hot

water for 5 minutes, then roughly chopped.

Handful fresh parsley

Handful fresh mint

Dressing

1 tbsp lemon juice

2 tbsp pomegranate molasses

1 tbsp extra virgin olive oil

Salt and black pepper

Method

Place the quinoa in plenty of water and bring to a gentle simmer for 12 -14 mins until it is tender. Drain and rinse with boiling water, then leave to stand in the colander for around 5 mins covered with a clean dry tea towel.

Meanwhile place the roasted vegetables in an ovenproof dish, scatter over the spices, olive oil, salt and black pepper, coating the vegetables thoroughly with the mixture. Roast in a pre-heated oven to 180 degrees for 40 mins, then turn up the oven to 200 degrees and roast for a further 10 mins until the vegetables are slightly caramelised.

Make the dressing by combining the pomegranate molasses, olive oil, lemon juice and season with salt and black pepper. Stir in the quinoa, roasted vegetables, dried cranberries and fresh herbs. Gently toss the ingredients to thoroughly coat with the dressing, finish by scattering over thc pumpkin seeds.

Serve with a spoonful of yogurt and a handful of fresh, crispy salad leaves.

A beautiful visualisation to raise your vibration

This a wonder to enjoy and is so relaxing and energising, perfect for lifting your energy frequency at any time of the day. Practised regularly it will help you in your spiritual journey of self-discovery.

I recommend that you record the script below, which will make it easier initially to practice.

Sit or lie comfortably, close your eyes, take a few deep breaths and allow your body and mind to relax.

Focus on your Earth Star Chakra, lying just below your feet and imagine that you are standing on a field of thousands of white lights, shining up so brightly illuminating your highest potential and possibilities for this life.

Lift your attention to your root and sacral chakras and imagine a beautiful, big diamond shining brightly from them, bringing you clarity and lighting up the path to your true destiny.

Now focus on your solar plexus chakra and imagine a ball of golden light radiating out to the universe and beyond. Bask in this ball of golden energy and in the feeling of safety, security and confidence that this golden light brings you. Know that you can return to this gorgeous golden light at any time of the day.

Visualise your heart chakra as vivid emerald green, now place your favourite beautiful white flower on top and imagine its soft petals opening one by one to the love of the universe. Imagine these soft petals receiving and giving love to the universe.

Bring your attention to your throat chakra and visualise a vibrant blue sapphire light shining out, surrounding you and protecting your entire body from any negative energy. Feel the security and protection that this blue light provides.

Lift your focus to your third eye chakra and allow an abundance of money, health and happiness to fill this chakra. Accept this abundance of all that you desire gratefully, knowing that you deserve all of it.

Lift your attention to your crown chakra and imagine a pure white light holding all the wisdom of the universe flooding into your crown chakra and flowing throughout your entire body.

Now visualise the place above your crown chakra and see a divine, feminine, white light shimmering down on you, like a shower of sparkling light, bringing a wonderful sense of peace and calm.

Now imagine a golden orange light filling your aura and radiating beyond, reaching the stars and universe.

When you are ready slowly open your eyes and take a few deep breaths, enjoying the feeling of peace, calm and security that this visualisation has given.

Rejuvenating roasted ratatouille

Affirmation

Every day in every way I feel youthful, enthusiastic and full of life.

Effect on the mind, body and soul

This dish is packed with vitamins, minerals and dietary fibre and will help rejuvenate and restore the body to a youthful balance. It has the potential to lower cholesterol, help manage weight and boost the immunity. The high levels of vitamin B and manganese will help with relaxation and balance stress.

Preparation

Labradorite is a powerful anti-ageing crystal, that not only prevents ageing, but also increases the production of youthful hormones such as elastin and collagen. Before you begin to prepare this recipe, place some labradorite at the centre of your table and you could even wear it as jewellery. Also, try energising your water by infusing it with this powerful gem and then sip the crystal water as you cook.

Ingredients

2 sweet potatoes peeled and cut into 1inch cubes

2 red onions peeled and sliced

1 courgette peeled and cubed

1 fennel bulb peeled and sliced

1 aubergine cubed

1 yellow pepper sliced

1 red pepper sliced

Salt and black pepper

2 tbsp olive oil

2 tsp dried oregano

Tomato Sauce

1 tbsp olive oil

3-4 cloves garlic

1 medium onion sliced

1 tbsp capers roughly chopped

1 tbsp organic raisins

1 tsp pine nuts

1 tbsp olives roughly chopped

A handful of fresh basil and parsley chopped

6 fresh tomatoes chopped

400g chopped organic tomatoes

1 tbsp balsamic vinegar

1 tsp organic brown sugar

Method

Place all the vegetables in a large, oven-proof dish, drizzle over the olive oil, scatter over the oregano, season with salt and black pepper. Then give a good stir to coat all the vegetables in the oil.

Place in the centre of a pre-heated oven to 180 degrees (fan 160 C/Gas 4) and roast for 40 mins or until all the vegetables have softened and very slightly caramelised.

Meanwhile make the sauce, by heating the oil and cooking the onions for around 10 minutes until they are softened and slightly caramelised, then add the garlic and salt stirring for a couple of minutes. Stir in the remaining ingredients, cover and cook gently for 20 minutes. Add the roasted vegetables to the sauce and stir gently to combine the ingredients. Cook for a further 5 minutes.

Delicious served with toasted pine nuts, green salad and garlic spelt bread.

Rejuvenating body balm

This natural organic balm is wonderfully repairing and rejuvenating for the body, it nourishes even the driest skin. So soothing, protecting and healing for aged and damaged skin.

Massage this relaxing balm into your skin, to calm a racing mind and anxious thoughts; it may even help alleviate menopause symptoms and bring down blood pressure!

The Neroli oil spiritually helps us to stay in the present moment and not reminisce of the past or even worry about the future. This healing balm helps us to connect to our divine destiny by energetically being in the moment

Ingredients

4 tbsp shea butter

2 tbsp coconut oil

2 tbsp jojoba oil

1 tbsp vitamin E

1 tbsp carrot seed oil

3 drops frankincense

3 drops rose

8 drops neroli

4 drops sandalwood

2 tbs organic aloe vera gel

Whip up the shea butter until it's mousse-like and then stir in the remaining ingredients. Store in a sterilised jar for up to 6 months

Be mindful when massaging this balm into your skin, focus on your affirmation and enjoy its healing properties.

Nutritionally packed red lentil, squash and sweet potato daal

Affirmation

I wake up feeling refreshed and energised and I allow this energy to remain with me all day.

Effect on the mind, body and soul

This is a delicious, richly nutritional meal which is packed with nutrients, vitamins and minerals, all providing impressive health benefits.

It's fabulous for boosting your immune system and for helping to protect the heart, lungs, eyes and bones.

It also has a wonderfully calming effect on the mind and body, for a more peaceful and contented life!

Preparation

Before eating, take a moment to sit quietly and visualise a healthy you, abundant with energy and confidence and surrounded by love. Then take a deep breath in and chant 'Hara hachi bu', three times, this reminds us to stop eating when our stomachs are 80% full, helping to prevent overloading our digestive systems which would deplete our energy leading us to feel tired and sluggish after eating.

Ingredients

1 tbsp coconut oil

5 cloves of garlic peeled and crushed

1 - 2 fresh red chillies, finely sliced

1 teaspoon black mustard seeds

1 heaped teaspoon cumin seeds

½ tsp fennel seeds

1 cinnamon stick

1 large onion peeled and finely sliced

2-inch piece of ginger, peeled and grated

1 bunch of fresh coriander finely chopped

1 small butternut squash peeled and diced into 2cm pieces

1 sweet potato peeled and diced into 2 cm pieces

2 fresh tomatoes chopped

200g organic split red lentils

1 tbsp double cream

3 tablespoons sheep's yoghurt

Juice from 1 lime

Salt and black pepper

Method

Gently heat the oil in a large, wide pan on medium heat. Throw in the mustard seeds, cumin seeds, fennel seeds, cinnamon stick and curry leaves and cook gently for a minute or two until the seeds start to pop, then add the onions and cook for around 10mins until soft and lightly golden.

Meanwhile blend the ginger, garlic, chilli and about a tablespoon of the fresh coriander stalks. Add the blend to the onions and cook gently, stirring constantly for a minute or two. Add a splash of water to prevent the ingredients from burning.

Then stir in the lentils, followed by the squash, sweet potato and tomatoes, add around 400 ml of stock or enough to cover generously. Bring to the boil, reduce to a gentle simmer and cover for 35 minutes, stirring occasionally. Spoon in the cream and half the lime juice, then fold in the chopped coriander. Season generously with salt and pepper.

Blend a handful of coriander leaves, the yoghurt, a pinch of sea salt and half the lime juice in a blender until smooth, then spoon into a small bowl.

Serve with the yogurt dressing, extra chopped coriander, poppadum's and a lime wedge or lime pickle and it's good with immune boosting coconut brown rice

Immune boosting coconut brown rice

Ingredients

200 ml brown basmati rice

1 tbsp organic desiccated coconut

1 tbsp chopped organic apricots

1 tbsp organic raisins

I cinnamon stick

1 star anise

1 tbsp coconut oil

½ tsp ground turmeric

A squeeze of lemon or lime juice

500 ml organic vegetable stock

Knob of butter

Method

Heat the oil and add the cinnamon and star anise, cooking for a minute of two. Stir in the rice and thoroughly coat with the oil, cook for a minute or two. Next add the dried fruit, turmeric and vegetable stock. Bring to a gentle simmer, add a knob of butter and put the lid on tightly and cook for 45 minutes or until all the stock has absorbed and the rice is cooked. Fluff with a fork and spoon over the toasted coconut and a good squeeze of lemon or lime juice.

Stir in a handful of fresh herbs, such as coriander, mint or parsley

The golden ball of energy visualisation

This is simple and easy to do at any time of the day, for a quick energy balancing fix. I like to practise it when I am lying in Savashana (corpse pose) before I begin my yoga postures. I find that I can then tap into this energy throughout my yoga practice and the rest of my day.

Relax in Savasana for a few minutes, become aware of the breath entering through your nostrils and out again. Now bring your attention to your earth star chakra, the area below your feet and visualise a bright, golden light shining there. Feel the energising warmth of this golden light on the soles of your feet, then visualise this cleansing, energising light spreading up into your legs, hips, belly and back. Now bring your attention to your fingers and bring this golden ball of light into your hands and feel it traveling up your arms to your neck, cleaning and energising. Allow the light to move into your head, bringing clarity and positivity. Now imagine that you are looking down at yourself and see yourself as this beautiful body of golden healing light. Know that this is your true self and that this energy will always be with you and that you can access it at any time.

Enjoy and when you're ready slowly open your eyes.

Healing and immune boosting thai squash soup

Affirmation

I feel the reassuring protective warmth of the universe, caring and nurturing me.

Effect on the mind, body and soul

This soup is not only delicious but also perfect for healing and nurturing the body, due to its wonderfully calming effect on the digestive system. Celery helps to restore the entire digestive system, so if you've been feeling a little anxious with butterflies in your tummy this is a lovely, healing soup for you.

It's perfect for lunch or a light supper as it's wonderful for nourishing the immunity and nervous systems; ginger and garlic are powerful immune boosters, butternut squash is a superfood, containing significant amounts of potassium and B6 and sweet potatoes are an amazing source of energy.

Spiritually, we often make life too complicated, creating anxiety, stress and tension, which in turn results in feeling out of balance and disconnected, depleting energy and vitality. This soup is protective and warming and reminds us of the importance of nurturing ourselves for peace and harmony.

Preparation

Take a moment to appreciate the healing energy of the ingredients before preparing the soup. Light a relaxing candle or incense stick and pop a few drops of frankincense oil and orange oil in a diffuser and play some relaxing music.

To further boost your immune system, place a drop of oregano oil in a glass of filtered water and sip as you prepare the recipe.

Ingredients

1 large organic butternut squash peeled cubed

4 organic carrots peeled and cubed

2 organic sweet potatoes peeled and cubed

1 large onion chopped

I stick organic celery, chopped

I can organic coconut cream

1 organic vegetable bouillon dissolved in 1 litre of water

4 cloves garlic chopped

1 large onion chopped

1-inch piece of ginger peeled

1 red chilli

1 stick lemongrass soaked

1 tbsp coconut oil

1 tbsp coconut syrup

Squeeze of lime juice

Handful of toasted pumpkin seeds

A spoonful of sheep's yogurt

Salt and black pepper

Fresh coriander to serve

Method

Gently fry the onion, celery, squash, carrots and sweet potatoes in a large ceramic saucepan for a minute. Meanwhile blend or finely chop the garlic, ginger, lemongrass and chilli and then add to the vegetables, giving a good stir.

Season with salt and put the lid on, turn the heat right down to the lowest setting and leave the vegetables for 30 minutes to gently stew.

Add the coconut cream, coconut syrup and vegetable stock, cook for 5 minutes or until the vegetables are softened, then blend to a puree. If the soup is too thick add a little more water or stock.

Serve with freshly chopped coriander, toasted pumpkin seeds, a spoonful of sheep's yogurt and a squeeze of lime juice

Nurturing and healing night oil

Affirmation

I am calm, relaxed and peaceful. I look forward to a restful night's sleep, waking refreshed and energised.

This beautiful, healing night oil not only nourishes the body but also calms the mind, body and soul for a restful night's sleep!

It is a powerful blend of natural ingredients, which all work to create a deeply balancing and calming effect on the emotions and mind. They also have a physical effect of toning and strengthening the body.

Frankincense has been used since ancient times spiritually, to uplift and to refine your sense of purpose. It helps to focus and clear the mind to overcome any stress and negativity.

It's perfect to use after soaking in a warm bath; massage a few drops into damp skin, repeating your affirmation, inhale deeply the aroma from your hands and visualise yourself restfully sleeping. To enhance the mood further, try lighting incense, dimming the lights and playing your favourite relaxing music.

Ingredients

45 ml camelia oil

10 ml vitamin E oil

4 drops lavender

3 drops camomile

4 drops bergamot

3 drops sandalwood

3 drops sweet orange

5 drops frankincense

Quartz crystal sterilised

Drop the crystal into a clean, sterilised, dark glass bottle, then add the oils and pop on the lid and shake the bottle to gently combine the oils.

Youth restoring roasted red peppers

Affirmation

I am happy, healthy and enthusiastic and full of youthful energy. I love life.

Effect on the mind, body and soul

This makes a delicious, very easy lunch or starter. It holds amazing benefits for your body; including helping to boost immunity, prevent cancer, improve eyesight, balance your mood and may even give you beautiful skin. Eat regularly to keep you feeling young and healthy!

It's perfect to eat if you're feeling stressed or under pressure, as the tomatoes help to lower blood pressure and have a calming effect on the nervous system. Eating light vegetarian dishes such as this one will raise your vibration, leaving you feeling happier and energised.

Preparation

The recipes below are packed with wonderful energising and youth restoring ingredients, take a moment to choose a couple of ingredients to hold in your hand and connect to their energy. Feeling gratitude, appreciation and understanding that they will nourish and energise your body.

Ingredients

6 red peppers halved and deseeded

3 medium tomatoes chopped

4-5 grilled artichokes roughly chopped

1 tbsp capers roughly chopped

1 tbsp basil thinly sliced

300ml organic feta cheese, diced

1 tbsp olives sliced

1 tbsp pine nuts

2 tbsp olive oil

Salt and black pepper

Method

Place the red peppers in an oven-proof dish. Season the inside with salt and drizzle with a little olive oil.

In a bowl, combine the tomatoes, artichokes, capers, basil, feta, olives and pine nuts.

Then stuff the peppers with this mixture. Season with a little salt and black pepper and then drizzle over the remaining olive oil.

Place in the centre of a pre-heated oven to 170

degrees (fan 150 C/Gas 3) for 50 mins

Delicious served with a crispy green salad, an aubergine salad and feta and yogurt sauce

Aubergine salad

1 aubergine cut into small dice

1 tbsp fresh mint chopped

1 tbsp fresh parsley chopped

1-2 tbsp olive oil

1 tbsp pomegranate molasses

Juice from 1 lemon

Method

Place the aubergine in an oven-proof dish, drizzle over 1 tbsp of olive oil, season with salt and pepper and then place in a hot oven 200 degrees for 30 mins.

Remove and gently stir in the herbs. Make a dressing with the lemon juice, pomegranate molasses and olive oil and then pour over the aubergine mixture.

Season with salt and pepper.

Feta and yogurt sauce

200 ml Greek yogurt

2 tomatoes roughly chopped

50 ml feta

1 garlic clove peeled and crushed

Black pepper

Squeeze lemon juice

Blend all the ingredients and serve with freshly chopped coriander. Delicious as a dip!

Youthful tip

Try sleeping with the anti-ageing crystal Mookaite Jasper, place it under your pillow to help slow down the ageing process. One of the reasons the body physically ages is because we believe that it is inevitable, the more you believe in the ageing process the more you physically age. The energy of this crystal changes these beliefs, it raises the vibration in your body and in your thoughts, helping you to feel younger in your attitude to life.

Rejuvenating serum

Fabulous for healing and toning the skin and for creating that beautiful, youthful glow. These natural ingredients work not only on improving the skin tone but also on uplifting and balancing the mind, body and soul

This is beautiful to use with a jade roller or Gua Sha jade massager.

Ingredients

5 ml aloe vera juice

10m raspberry seed oil

5ml pomegranate oil

5ml carrot seed oil

5ml chia seed oil

15ml rosehip oil

5 ml hyaluronic serum

5 drops sandalwood

6 drops frankincense

3 drops jasmine

5 drops neroli

3 drops rose

Combine all the ingredients in a serialised glass bottle.

Protecting superfood salmon, two ways

Affirmation

I am in perfect health and every day I nourish and take care of my body.

Effect on the mind, body and soul

Salmon has impressive health benefits from nurturing the heart and brain to preventing some major diseases. These recipes teach you that it is important to take care and nourish your body and by doing so, not only are you helping to balance your mind and soul but most important of all, to give yourself the gift of love.

Preparation

Prepare these dishes with love; love for yourself, for family, friends, animals, for the universe and life itself.

Focus for a minute or two on your heart chakra, visualising the opening of the petals of your favourite white flower, opening to the love of the universe. Place a bunch of your favourite flowers in your kitchen or on your dining room table, put on the music you love to listen to and enjoy preparing and cooking these dishes.

Protecting superfood salmon, the first way

Ingredients

4 wild or organic salmon fillets

I tbsp sesame seeds

1 tbsp fresh coriander

Knob of butter

I tbsp ground nut oil

Marinade

1 tbsp tamari

1 tbsp sweet chilli sauce

1 tsp sesame oil

1 tsp grated ginger

1 tbsp lemon juice

1 tsp brown rice vinegar

Method

Pre heat the oven to 180 degrees (fan 160 C/Gas 4)

Whisk together the marinade ingredients and then combine thoroughly with the salmon, leaving to marinade for an hour or so.

In a shallow frying pan heat the oil, then keeping

the heat high, brown the salmon quickly on both sides and pop in a pre-heated oven for 5 mins or until cooked through.

Delicious with stir-fried vegetables

Protecting superfood salmon, the second way

Ingredients

4 wild or organic salmon fillets

4-5 sprigs of fresh tarragon finely chopped

1 tbsp white wine

Squeeze of lemon

Salt and black pepper

12 fresh cherry tomatoes

Knob of butter

1 tbsp olive oil

1 bulb of fennel thinly sliced

1 tbsp capers

Serve with:

Caper crème fraiche sauce

200 ml organic crème fraiche

1 tbsp chopped capers

1 tsp Dijon mustard

1 tsp finely chopped fresh parsley

Salt and black pepper

Squeeze lemon juice

Method

Gently heat the oil in a shallow frying pan and add the sliced fennel, cook gently for 5 minutes until the fennel just begins to soften. Then add the capers, white wine and tarragon and set the mixture aside.

Place the salmon fillets in a buttered, oven-proof dish and then spoon over the fennel mixture. Scatter over the cherry tomatoes, season with salt and black pepper, then add a couple of knobs of butter and pop in the centre of a pre-heated oven to 180 degrees (fan 160 C/Gas 4) for 20 mins.

Delicious served with a crisp green salad.

Super nutrient face mask to protect your skin

Fabulous rejuvenating mask for an amazing pick-me-up and hydration.

Papaya is packed with anti-oxidants and full of alpha-hydroxy acid. Yogurt is a natural probiotic and honey encourages moisture in the skin without triggering excess oil, and it is also a skin lightener, as is lemon, so it's great for blemishes and dark spots. Avocado and coconut oil are extremely effective moistures and perfect for dry skin. Egg white is a natural facelift, tightening the skin and rich in vitamin A.

Ingredients

1 tbsp ripe papaya

1 tbsp ripe avocado

1 tsp raw honey

1 teaspoon fresh lemon juice

1 free range egg white

1 tbsp sheep's yogurt

Raw coconut oil

3 drops frankincense oil

Mash the papaya and avocado, then add the honey, lemon juice, egg white, yogurt, coconut oil and frankincense oil. Stir thoroughly to combine all the ingredients, then carefully apply to a cleansed face. Leave on for at least 20 minutes, then gently wash off all the ingredients.

Abundance-giving vegetable and nut curry

Affirmation

I deserve wealth and prosperity and all that I ask for I will receive.

Effect on the mind, body and soul

This recipe is a powerhouse of nutrition, every ingredient has healing benefit to the mind, body and soul. I recommend cooking this delicious recipe, whenever you feel that your body is low in immunity and needs some extra support. It's wonderful at boosting your energy and balancing your mind, body and soul.

Preparation

Prepare with gratitude and the understanding that you can attract abundance into your life. Take a moment to repeat the affirmation and then set a clear intention on what you want to attract into your life; such as wealth, health, happiness, love.

Decorate your table with a beautiful, green jade crystal, used since ancient times to bring wealth and prosperity and chrysanthemums or tulips to represent abundant joy and a long, fruitful life.

Ingredients

1 medium organic cauliflower cut into small florets

1 medium head of organic broccoli cut into small florets

150 g frozen peas

A couple of handfuls of fresh organic spinach, roughly chopped

1 large onion sliced

1 tbsp coconut oil

1 tin of organic coconut milk

1 level tsp mustard seeds

1 level tsp cumin seeds

½ tsp garam masala

2-3 fresh tomatoes cut into quarters

Salt

1 tbsp agave syrup or coconut sugar

Juice from half lemon

50 mil organic vegetable stock or filtered water

Handful of fresh coriander

Paste

50g desiccated coconut, organic if possible

2 tbsp cashew nuts

1 tbsp sesame seeds

I inch ginger, peeled

2-3 cloves garlic peeled

1cm turmeric root, peeled

1-2 fresh hot green chilli

3-4 tbsp filtered water

Salt

Method

In a small frying pan, dry roast the coconut for a minute or two, stirring frequently until it's slightly browned, then place in a blender. Then add the sesame seeds and as soon as they start to pop, put in them in the blender. Add the oil and stir-fry the cashew nuts until they are slightly brown and add them to the blender. Then add the ginger, garlic, turmeric, chilli, water and salt and blend to a paste.

Meanwhile, heat the oil and add the mustard seeds and cumin seeds, as soon as they start popping, turn the heat down and add the onion and cook gently for around 5 minutes until softened and slightly caramelised. Add the paste and cook gently for a few minutes to release the flavours, follow by the cauliflower and broccoli, giving a good stir to thoroughly coat the vegetables in the paste. Stir in the coconut milk, water, garam masala, lemon juice and agave syrup, bring to a gentle simmer and then add the tomatoes. Pop on a lid and simmer gently for 10-15 minutes, until the vegetables are just tender. Then stir in the peas and spinach and cook for a further 2-3 minutes. Season with salt and black pepper. Serve with a few handfuls of freshly chopped coriander.

Serve with:

Healing tamarind fried rice

Ingredients

300g brown basmati rice

2 tbsp tamarind paste

200ml water, filtered if possible

1 tbsp coconut oil

1tsp cumin seeds

1 tsp black mustard seeds

1 tsp chilli flakes

1 tbsp desiccated coconut

2cm piece root ginger, finely grated

2 cloves garlic, finely grated

1 onion sliced

Method

Begin by cooking the rice in boiling, slightly salted water, then drain and refresh with boiling water, then set aside.

Put the tamarind paste and the water into a pan and bring to a gentle simmer for a couple of minutes, then remove from the heat.

In a shallow pan, heat the oil and sprinkle in the mustard seeds, cumin seeds and chilli flakes, fry for a minute until fragrant and popping. Then add the onion and cook until softened and slightly caramelised, stir in the ginger, garlic and cabbage and stir-fry for a couple of minutes until slightly soft and slight browned. Add the desiccated coconut, tamarind water, then finally the rice. Give a stir and cook for 2-3 mins until the rice is piping hot.

Visualisation for attracting wealth

Sit or lie comfortably and close your eyes, softening your gaze up to your Ajna or third eye chakra. Take a couple of deep inhalations and as you exhale, release any tension you may be holding onto. Then let your breath go and allow it to gently and easily flow through your nostrils. Now bring your attention back to your third eye chakra and visualise breathing in and exhaling a soft luminescence or radiance, like the light of the moon. After a few breaths, visualise filling this chakra with wealth and abundance, allowing all that you desire; wealth, love, happiness, health, prosperity to flood into your Ajna. Willingly accept all these gifts, knowing that you are worthy and that you deserve them.

relax,
calm
down
your mind,
smile
inside
and be happy

A Message from the Author

Dear Reader,

I hope that you have enjoyed reading this book and that it has inspired you to change the way you view food. I trust that you are now feeling the benefit of the affirmations, yoga and use of crystals, accompanying the healing recipes and that you have already begun to feel their positive, healing effects.

With love, light and happiness.

- Anna Howard

"To keep the body in good health is a duty ... otherwise, we shall not be able to keep our mind strong and clear."

\- Buddha

Available worldwide from Amazon

---

https://mtp.agency

https://facebook.com/mtp.agency

@mtp_agency